P9-EJH-330

TWAYNE'S WORLD AUTHORS SERIES

A Survey of the World's Literature

Sylvia E. Bowman, Indiana University

GENERAL EDITOR

SPAIN

Gerald Wade, Vanderbilt University

EDITOR

Ramón Del Valle-Inclán

(TWAS 160)

TWAYNE'S WORLD AUTHORS SERIES (TWAS)

The purpose of TWAS is to survey the major writers—novelists, dramatists, historians, poets, philosophers, and critics—of the nations of the world. Among the national literatures covered are those of Australia, Canada, China, Eastern Europe, France, Germany, Greece, India, Italy, Japan, Latin America, the Netherlands, New Zealand, Poland, Russia, Scandinavia, Spain, and the African nations, as well as Hebrew, Yiddish, and Latin Classical literatures. This survey is complemented by Twayne's United States Authors Series and English Authors Series.

The intent of each volume in these series is to present a critical-analytical study of the works of the writer; to include biographical and historical material that may be necessary for understanding, appreciation, and critical appraisal of the writer; and to present all material in clear, concise English—but not to vitiate the scholarly content of the work by doing so.

Ramón Del Valle-Inclán

By VERITY SMITH

Westfield College
(University of London)

Twayne Publishers, Inc.   ::   New York

For Tracy and Francesca

Preface

It is my purpose in this study to provide a brief guide to Valle-Inclán's literary production, hoping that it will serve at the same time as a summary of recent criticism which has shed new light on the author's output. Given the nature of this study, an overall picture of Valle-Inclán's art, I have found it desirable to concentrate on what seems to be his most rewarding period, that of his later years. Although the trend has been reversed recently, much more attention has been given to works of the *modernista* phase, such as the *Sonatas,* than is warranted by their merits. Since this introduction to the works of Valle-Inclán is of necessity brief, it will prove impossible to consider every interesting point in detail. Consequently, it will be my purpose, both in footnotes and in the bibliography, to provide information about more comprehensive works to be consulted by readers whose interest has been aroused in any one particular aspect of the writer's production.

During the past few years there has been a significant change in the approach to Valle-Inclán's works. What has emerged very clearly is a determination to come to grips with the fundamental thoughts underlying his production. Formerly critics had tended to concentrate on three purely external aspects of Valle's output to the detriment of other equally (if not more) important features. These were a) his debt to other writers, much being said in shocked and sanctimonious tones about his weakness for plagiarizing material; b) his style, bound to arouse interest since the texture of his prose is inordinately rich, full of verbal pyrotechnics and a use of words that evidences a remarkably sensitive and musical ear; c) anecdotes about the writer concerning his withering barbs, brushes with the Spanish authorities, his bizarre appearance, and so forth. The last is perhaps the most deplorable as it tended to exaggerate interest in the idiosyncrasies of the man at the expense of the writer.

Now, instead, attention is being focused on Valle-Inclán's esthetics, the genesis of his works, and his political ideology. It is these more fundamental aspects which are my main concern in the present study, written especially for the reader who may be unaware of the often complex thought underlying his work.

One aspect of Valle's work to which I shall be devoting some attention is his interest in theosophy and esoteric Christian heresies such as Gnosticism. This search for spiritual revelation through his initiation into occult lore links the author with a number of artists from the Symbolists onwards. It is a quest for absolute truth by irrational and intuitive methods which reveals the artist's disenchantment with materialist philosophies of the second half of the nineteenth century such as Positivism and Determinism. It should be added, however, that Valle was by nature a dabbler and a dilettante and that his approach to the question of esoteric cults, as to certain other matters, did not necessarily involve serious study. In point of fact, any kind of scholarly approach to background material is something Valle would have scorned, although an exception must be made of his attitude in a cycle of historical novels planned in the 1920's under the general title of *El ruedo ibérico (The Iberian Ring)*. In general, as the author himself declared, he preferred to deal with characters who already had an established and recognizable background such as a beggar, or Job. Such archetypes are related to Platonic Forms or Ideas: the beggar and Job are the very distillation of wretchedness and suffering. Valle-Inclán's interest in aspects of Plato's philosophy is something which has as yet elicited little attention from students of Valle's works. Consequently it is a question which will be considered in this study.

If I were to summarize in a phrase Valle-Inclán's development as a writer, it would be to say that his work involved one assertion and two negations. The positive element is to be found in Valle-Inclán's political ideology which, in my opinion, remained unchanged from the start to the very end of his literary career. Valle felt a strong emotional attachment for the extreme Right, that is, for the Carlists. But its expression in the two periods into which his work is normally divided, namely that of

Modernismo and that of the *esperpento,* is negative. In the earlier *modernista* phase he deliberately takes refuge in an artificial world of his own devising in which the Carlist values so dear to him are treated with due reverence; in the works of the *esperpento* period, when the earlier false vision has been discarded and the author takes stock of his country as it really is—at least to his jaundiced eyes—he lashes out and destroys what he sees before him. Thus his approach in both instances is negative: in the earlier works Valle wilfully turns his back on the Spanish society of his period so as to create a Carlist utopia in which the plebs gladly accept a subservient position. In the later novels he takes stock of Spanish society, but only to satirize, vilify and reject it, clinging to the Carlist values he holds dear, although he is aware that the times are out of joint for such a retrogressive system of government to be acceptable.

This negative attitude to Spanish society is the underlying element in all his major works. It gives them unity and cohesion despite the contradictory aesthetics which would appear to distinguish the earlier from the later works.

Before ending I wish to express my gratitude to my colleague Alan Deyermond for his constructive criticisms of my manuscript. In addition I should mention that the translations of all the titles of Valle-Inclán's works as of passages quoted from the texts are my own. A number of these are rather free renderings, since my feeling was, and remains, that the author himself would have seen fit where necessary to sacrifice accuracy on the altar of style.

Author's Note

This book was written in 1966 and 1967. Owing to circumstances beyond my control its publication has been delayed by a matter of years. Whilst the bibliography has been brought up to date, it would have proved impossible short of completely rewriting this study to have incorporated more recent critical material into the text.

Contents

Chronology

1866   Valle-Inclán born at Villanueva de Arosa in the province of Pontevedra, Galicia.

1888   Starts law studies at University of Santiago de Compostela.

1885-
1890   Spends some time in Madrid where he writes articles and short stories for the Liberal newspaper *El Globo* and the magazine *La Ilustración Ibérica*.

1892   First visit to Mexico.

1895   Publication of *Femeninas (Feminine Cameos)*.

1896-
1897   Settles definitively in Madrid.

1902   Publication of *Sonata de otoño (Autumn Sonata)*.

1903   Publication of *Sonata de estío (Summer Sonata)* and two collections of short stories, *Corte de amor (Court of Love)* and *Jardín umbrío (The Shaded Garden)*.

1904   Publication of *Sonata de primavera (Spring Sonata)* and *Flor de santidad (Saintly Flower)*.

1905   Appearance of the last Sonata, *Invierno (Winter)*.

1907   Marries the actress Josefina Blanco. Publishes *Aguila de blasón (The Eagle Scutcheon)*.

1907-
1908   Visits Navarre where he meets veterans of the second Carlist War and gathers material for his novels concerning this period of Spanish history.

1908   Publication of *Romance de lobos (The Ballad of the Wolves)* and *Los cruzados de la causa (The Crusaders of the Cause)*.

1908-
1909   Publication of two novels concerning the second Carlist

war, *El resplandor de la hoguera (The Bonfire's Glow)* and *Gerifaltes de antaño (Gerfalcons of Yore)*.

1909 Two farces, *La cabeza del dragón (The Dragon's Head)* and *Cuento de abril (April Story)*, are staged at the Teatro de la Comedia in Madrid.

1909-
1910 Stands as candidate for Spanish *Cortes* representing Traditionalist party.

1912 Two plays staged in Madrid, *Voces de gesta (Epic Voices)* and *La marquesa Rosalinda (Lady Rosalind)*.

1914 Publication of a much expanded edition of *Jardín umbrío.*

1916 Visits French front as correspondent for Madrid newspaper *El Imparcial.* Publishes *La lámpara maravillosa (The Wonderful Lamp)*. In July is appointed Professor of Esthetics at Madrid School of Fine Arts.

1917 Publication of *La media noche (At Midnight)*, the result of his observations at the allied front in France.

1919 Appearance of the verse collection *La pipa de kif (The Marihuana Pipe)*.

1920 Undergoes surgery. This marks the start of his long struggle against the illness of which he was finally to die.

1920 Publication of two plays in contrasting veins, *Farsa de la enamorada del rey (The Farce of the Maid who Loved a King)* and *Divinas palabras (Divine Words)*.

1921 Second visit to Mexico where he attends the Independence celebrations.

1923 Publication of the third part of the trilogy *Comedias bárbaras (The Vandals), Cara de plata (Silver Face)*.

1924 Appearance of the *esperpento Luces de bohemia (Bohemian Lights)*.

1925 Publishes *Los cuernos de don Friolera (Don Friolera's Horns)*.

1926 *Tirano Banderas (The Tyrant)*.

1927 *La corte de los milagros (The Court of Miracles)*.

1928 *Viva mi dueño (Hurrah for My Owner)*.

1930 Publication of three *esperpentos* under title of *Martes de carnaval (Shrove Tuesday)*.

1932 Faced a severe financial setback owing to bankruptcy of his publishers. In the same year the Madrid newspaper

El Sol begins to serialize his novel *Bazas de espadas (Military Tricks)*. Divorces his wife.

1933   Appointed director of the Spanish Academy of Fine Arts in Rome by the Republican government. Starts contributing articles to newspaper *Ahora*.

1935   Resigns appointment because of ill health and enters a clinic run by his friend Dr. Villar Iglesias in Santiago de Compostela.

1936   Dies on January 5.

CHAPTER 1

Valle-Inclán's Life and Times

R AMÓN VALLE PEÑA[1] was born in the small fishing village
of Villanueva de Arosa, province of Pontevedra, in October, 1866. In common with many members of the "Generation
of 1898"—with whom his literary connections are a matter of
controversy—the subject of this study belonged, as a native of
Spain's most northwesterly province—Pontevedra is in Galicia—
to a peripheral region of Spain. As was also the case with Unamuno, Baroja and Azorín, all three non-Castilians, Valle's interest
was to center on Castile, although in his case this development
occurred rather late in life. It is the Galician background that
is an important factor in a number of his earlier works,[2] and for
this reason, although he evidently transcends the regional, this
earlier interest is worth considering in some detail.

In Galicia the Celtic influence is evident not only in the wealth
of archeological remains but also in a religion which, although
on the surface of an orthodox Roman Catholic order, has, underlying it, a strong pagan foundation. It will become evident in
the course of this study that Valle-Inclán had a marked proclivity
for juxtaposing Christian with pagan—usually sensual—material.
A further legacy of the Celts is the number of legends, superstitions and mythological characters which have survived the
passage of time and on which the author draws, particularly in
his earlier short stories.[3] It is worth observing that even the
author's more mature works bear witness to his undying fascination for the folklore of his native region.

Also worth taking into account in regard to his Galician environment are the social changes resulting from the rise of the
Spanish middle class in the nineteenth century. The rural gentry
of Galicia, for which Valle felt a marked affinity, was in a state

of decline owing in part to altered social circumstances. The position of these traditional *hidalgos* in a society which provided them with ever less scope for their talents, while at the same time reducing their privileges, had emerged as a preoccupation among certain writers of the previous generation, such as José María Pereda and Emilia Pardo Bazán. The latter had shown her concern for the social and moral decline of the Galician squirearchy in her most famous novel *Los pazos de Ulloa (The Manors of Ulloa)*. Nor was this preoccupation limited to Spain: beyond the Pyrenees Barbey d'Aurevilly dwelt sorrowfully on the straitened circumstances of the French provincial aristocracy.[4] And Baudelaire, attacking on a wider front, vented his spleen on the increasingly bourgeois-oriented society in which it was his misfortune to live, devising, to counteract it, his own version of the dandy.[5] Valle not only shared this concern, but felt passionately involved in the matter. He considered himself a spiritual descendant of this very section of the population menaced by decay and possible extinction, stripped of their former status and left to molder in provincial backwaters.

Linked with his belief in an outdated social order, and coupled with a profound scorn for an increasingly egalitarian society, is Valle's adherence to Carlism. The Carlists, or Traditionalists as they were to become, occupied the extreme right of the political spectrum: political reactionaries who in the nineteenth century still countenanced the Divine Right of Kings, the active participation of the Church in State affairs and a hierarchical social order.[6] Thus they held out to the provincial squirearchy—from whom they drew a great deal of support—the hope of recovering their former position as unchallenged lords of the manor caring, with a spirit of benevolent paternalism, for the peasants on their lands and held in high esteem, if not awe, by civic and church dignitaries in the area.

From this brief outline of the ideal society as envisaged by Valle-Inclán in his earlier works, it becomes apparent that at least where political leanings are concerned it is unwise to connect him—as Hans Jescke and Pedro Laín have done—[7] with the so-called-generation of '98. In the 1890's Unamuno looked on himself as a Marxist; Azorín as an Anarchist, whilst both they, Baroja and Maeztu militated for social reforms and sought remedies for the mental and spiritual stagnation of their countrymen. Valle, on the other hand, buried his head in the sand like the traditional ostrich and refused to come to terms with the unpalatable facts.

There are no detailed accounts of Valle's childhood, but there is little reason to presume that it was anything other than tranquil and normal. Indeed, so far as the natural environment was concerned, it was nothing short of idyllic. The first circumstance of interest to the literary critic is Valle's departure in 1885 to Santiago de Compostela where he began to study law, a subject then virtually *de rigueur* for the sons of prosperous Spaniards. At this juncture it is worth mentioning one minor point of contact with Azorín, Unamuno and Baroja, namely that the university course Valle followed failed to provide him with any form of stimulus whatsoever.[8] However, this period was not totally unproductive because it was here that he began to read widely, absorbing the works of certain contemporary French authors and acquainting himself with the philosophy of Plato which was in time to affect his maturer works. It was also while at Santiago that Valle began contributing short stories to local literary magazines, and it was there also that he embarked on a novel to be entitled *El gran obstáculo (The Great Obstacle)* of which only fragments are extant.

After leaving the university without a degree, Valle spent some time in Madrid where he wrote articles and short stories for the Liberal newspaper *El Globo*. Subsequently, in 1892, he made his first visit to Mexico. He is said to have picked Mexico at random because it was written with an "x." Although this witticism may be apocryphal, it reflects the studied nonchalance he was to adopt in literature through his alter ego, the Marqués de Bradomín. During his stay in Mexico Valle earned his living as a journalist, writing short stories and articles for two newspapers, *El Correo Español* and *El Universal*. The articles refer in the main to Spain, some being concerned with literary and political figures of the period, while in others he dwells on the more picturesque aspects of his native Galicia.[9] A few of the short stories published in Mexico, such as "Caritativa" ("The Charitable Singer") and "El canario" ("The Canary"), were to be republished at a later date in Spain, with interesting stylistic modifications. One of the more significant of his publications in Mexico was "Bajo los trópicos: 1. En el mar" ("Under a Tropic

Sky: 1. At Sea"). It contains a description of the bay of Veracruz
to be found in the later "La niña Chole" ("The Mexican Princess"), in itself a primitive draft of the more ambitious *Sonata de
estío (Summer Sonata)* in which the same description appears
yet again.[10]

Valle-Inclán returned to Spain in the early months of 1893.
From this time until his departure for Madrid in 1895 little is
known of his activities in literary or other spheres. Until more
facts concerning this period of his life come to light, one must
presume that he led the life of a young man of leisure with
literary inclinations, residing with his family in Pontevedra, in-
creasing his knowledge of contemporary fiction,[11] and putting
the last touches to the manuscript of *Femeninas (Feminine Cameos)*, a collection of short stories published in Pontevedra
early in 1895.

By April 1895 Valle had established himself, this time definitively, in the capital. Here, with very little money and no financial
prospects to speak of, he led a bohemian existence alternating
between seedy lodgings and long periods of debate and heated
discussion in the cafés of Madrid frequented by both aspiring
and established men of letters. It was in this way that he came to
meet young writers such as Martínez Ruiz (Azorín), the Baroja
brothers, Benavente, Rubén Darío and "household names" such
as Palacio Valdés. These contacts were to prove stimulating and,
indirectly, to affect his work since it was at this time that Valle
began to write in the *modernista* vein—as is palpably clear from
the volume *Epitalamio (Epithalamium)* which appeared in 1897.
He also continued to read the works of writers commonly associated with the *fin de siècle* atmosphere such as D'Annunzio,
Huysmans and Wilde. In one way, however, a café was to prove
his undoing, since as the result of a mundane brawl in one of his
haunts a very minor flesh wound became infected and, finally,
his left arm had to be amputated.

Valle-Inclán's deep-rooted and abiding interest in the theater—
as apparent in his personal behavior as in the dramatic bias of
his production—found its first concrete outlet in 1898 when he
took the part of a bizarre *modernista* poet called Teófilo Everit
in one of Benavente's early social satires *La comida de las fieras
(Feeding Time at the Zoo)*. Apparently he was deeply wounded
by the critics' cool reaction to his performance and abandoned

the rôle in a fit of pique after only a few appearances.[12] In the following year a very mediocre play *Cenizas (Ashes)*,[13] which owes all too much to the *comedias burguesas* of the then popular dramatist Echegaray, received an equally cool reception from the critics. This experience would seem to have damped his ardor to write for the theater since he was not to cultivate the dramatic form again for some years.

Valle's first major achievement in the *modernista* manner was *Sonata de otoño (Autumn Sonata)*, published in 1902,[14] closely followed by the *Summer, Spring* and *Winter* ones. The year 1904 marked the publication not only of *Sonata de primavera (Spring Sonata)* but also of *Flor de santidad (Saintly Flower)*, an elaboration of an earlier short story, "Adega" (1899).[15]

In 1907 the author married an actress, Josefina Blanco, who a year before had played a part in his play *El marqués de Bradomín (The Marquis of Bradonín)*, a sentimentalized pastiche of the *Sonatas* in which he also inserted snippets from other works of the period. The couple were to have six children, of whom five reached maturity. Towards the end of 1907 Valle travelled to Navarre to document himself on the background and the military maneuvers of the second Carlist War (1872-1876), being at this time engaged on a trilogy of novels about this period in Spanish history. In Navarre he met veterans of the Northern campaigns and covered on foot the terrain where battles and skirmishes had taken place. Simultaneously, Valle was engaged on another trilogy, this time of novels in dialogue in which he concentrated entirely on the subject which at this time engrossed and moved him like none other: the provincial aristocracy of Galicia and its economic and moral decline.

The year 1909 marked the revival of the author's interest in the stage with the production of two light-hearted, stylized plays, *Farsa de la cabeza del dragón (The Farce of the Dragon's Head)* and *Cuento de abril (April Story)*. It is possible that he turned to these plays for light relief while still engaged on the trilogies in which his emotions were so deeply involved. Later in the same year the author accompanied his wife who was under contract to the theatrical company directed by Francisco García Ortega on a tour of certain Latin-American countries. Their first engagement was in the Canary Isles after which they took ship for Argentina. In Buenos Aires Valle-Inclán gave four lectures, these being "Stimulants," "The Art of Writing," "Modernismo," and "The Spain of Yesteryear." It is to be regretted that no transcripts were taken at the time, with the result that the critic has to rely on the summaries given in local newspapers.

In the lecture on Hispanic Modernism Valle showed a dislike of what he termed "a newspaper literature now in vogue." Emotion, he told his audience, should not be confused with sentimentality. Such views are to be given very forceful expression in his works of the nineteen-twenties. "The Art of Writing" is another lecture whose content hints at that of a future work. Here Valle attacks the Spanish "classic" manner of writing which, he says, stultifies the language. This is a point on which he was to elaborate in *The Wonderful Lamp*.

On their return to Spain, Valle made an unsuccessful bid to secure his election to the Spanish *Cortes* as a candidate for the Traditionalist party in the district of Monforte de Lemus. Thwarted in his attempt to participate actively in the political party of his choice, Valle devoted an entire work to the subject of Carlism for the last time in his life. On this occasion the work in question was in dramatic form. *Voces de gesta (Epic Voices)* is a play of inferior quality which was published in 1911 and received its first performance a year later.

In 1912 Valle-Inclán decided to move with his family from Madrid and to take up permanent residence in Galicia. This action may have been inspired by his economic situation, which was seldom secure for long periods. Again, he may have hankered after the stability provided by a familiar and much loved setting at a time when, as a writer, and perhaps also as an individual, he seems rather disorientated. Few are the works published in the following three or four years of his life and those he did produce are evidently escapist in character. These, in my view, are the barren years when, having purged his soul of the two fundamental preoccupations of his earlier works, namely Carlism and the circumstances of the Galician squirearchy, and having outgrown the *modernista* credo, Valle needed a respite in which to rethink his position as a writer. The works of this period are *La marquesa Rosalinda (Lady Rosalind)* and *El embrujado (A Man Bewitched)*, both published in 1913, and *La lámpara maravillosa (The Wonderful Lamp)*, published in 1916. The last-mentioned work reflects his spiritual restlessness and insecurity. It is concerned with aspects of mystical revelation; the beliefs of the Gnostics and the initiates of other esoteric cults, as though the writer is searching for a new faith to fill the vacuum left by Carlism and the aristocratic ideals which he had now, to some extent, outgrown. 1916 was to prove a climacteric in Valle-Inclán's life. In that year he travelled to France to see something of the Western Front after being commissioned for a series of articles on the progress of the war by the well-established Madrid newspaper *El Imparcial*.

It had emerged clearly in certain passages from the *Sonata de invierno (Winter Sonata)* as well as the *Carlist War* trilogy that Valle, perhaps in the shadow of Nietzsche, had praised the cruelty and atavism which are the inevitable corollaries of war. The devastated countryside of Northern France; the squalor and misery resulting from trench warfare; the loss of life on a tragic and unprecedented scale, must have provided the most bitterly ironic comment on his naïve and idealized vision of war and warriors. The revulsion and the sorrow he felt when confronted with the truth about modern warfare and its effects on mankind are to be found in *La media noche (At Midnight)*, which he elaborated from jottings made at the front itself and from the articles written for *El Imparcial*.

In 1919, Valle published a collection of poems called *La pipa de kif (The Marihuana Pipe)* which heralds a completely new style of writing to culminate later in the *esperpentos*. The new style is coupled with an apparent change of attitude towards Spanish society. Such a drastic revision of his former position both as man and artist—if indeed it is as fundamental as appears at first glance—cannot be attributed to one reason alone but, rather, to a number of them. In the first place, it would seem that by the second decade of the century Valle-Inclán realized that he had exhausted the possibilities of the *modernista* esthetic and that the reading public was growing weary of its outdated trappings. Rebellion and change were in the air as much in the visual arts as in literature, in France, Germany and Italy. Of course, some of the "isms" of the period such as Expressionism, Cubism and Futurism had been formulated and put into practice before the outbreak of the Great War. But the war itself, responsible for toppling the old social order, acted as a catalyst, allowing revolu-

tionary art movements to take root and become rather more than
mere seven-day wonders.

Valle-Inclán, as I shall hope to show in the following chapter,
was very sensitive to movements and trends in the arts and readily
embraced the revolutionary cause. As an artist of fastidious taste
he chose with discrimination, not adhering to the tenets of any
one movement but, instead, adopting an eclectic outlook. Furthermore, he adapted these external stimuli to suit his own talents,
thus producing works which bear at one and the same time the
hallmark of the period while remaining very much his own personal creation. It is very difficult, and this is to his credit, to
speak of a particular movement in the arts which exercised a
decesive influence on him. In this way Valle succeeded where
his contemporaries the *ultraístas* failed,[16] for he was able to fuse
together elements from various avant-garde movements creating
a harmonious and original whole.

Certain events in the sphere of Spanish politics should be
mentioned at this point because they served to increase his disillusionment with war and warriors, more particularly the latter.
Spain's loss of Cuba and the Philippines after the Spanish-
American war of 1898 did not put an end to the country's over-
seas commitments, for there remained the thorny problem of
North Africa. An agreement reached with the French in 1912
confirmed certain Spanish responsibilities in the area which had
first been proposed in 1906, and had resulted in the establish-
ment of a Spanish protectorate in the Northwestern zone of
Morocco. For years the country, already bedevilled by grave
political problems on the home front, had to contend also with
the pacification of the zone, a task rendered all the more difficult
because the Rif tribesmen had found a very able leader in Abd-
el-Krim. In 1921 King Alfonso XIII, acting with wanton stupidity,
was responsible for a campaign led by a general whom he favored, Silvestre by name, which resulted in a series of unprecedented disasters. Such was the public outcry—for when evolving
the harebrained scheme the King had consulted neither the
Minister of War nor the Commander-in-Chief of the North
African forces—that Alfonso was forced to consent to an official
enquiry into the causes of the disaster. The facts that emerged
revealed a frighteningly high degree of incompetence and irre-
sponsibility among senior officers.[17]

To hush up his own part in the tragedy, Alfonso was forced to turn to the army for help and to condone the military dictatorship of Primo de Rivera, which was to last until 1930. Although he was a controversial figure, it would be wrong to condemn Primo de Rivera out of hand. For example, he successfully came to terms with the Rif tribesmen; he started a program of road building and modernization of the railways and was enlightened in his dealings with the militant trade unions. But, as Salvador de Madariaga points out, the record of the dictatorship, generally good in material reforms, was detrimental to the intellectual and spiritual life of the nation. Particularly suspect were the records of the Department of the Interior and the Ministries of Education and Justice.[18] Furthermore, the regime made itself very unpopular with intellectuals because the press was censored and liberty of speech suppressed. In his attitude to the dictatorship, Valle was no exception, and although unlike Unamuno he avoided exile, he did have more than one brush with the authorities and was loud in his protests at the abuses for which he held the government responsible. Granted this background, it is not difficult to appreciate why Valle-Inclán should have treated the military with such acerbity in his later works. A certain degree of reaction from his former position would have been natural anyway, but his complete volte-face is accounted for by the glaring faults of the military in the later years of his life.

Increasingly, Valle was to veer from the Right to the Left in politics, although it is difficult to determine just how sincere was this change of ideology which on the surface is as radical as his change of style. The truth is that Valle's political outlook in old age is rather ambiguous, and his frequent use of irony makes it well-nigh impossible to reach any definite conclusion on the subject. The one categorical statement I am prepared to make is that to the very end of his life he bitterly resented the status quo, seeing in it the triumph of all that was mediocre and unenlightened in Spanish society. Perhaps in addition, as Avalle Arce maintains,[19] he saw in Traditionalism and Anarchism alternative routes of escape, since both movements offered solutions to the democratic farce which had culminated in a military dictatorship.

In 1921 the Mexican scholar and diplomat Alfonso Reyes extended an invitation to the author to attend the celebrations organized in the Mexican capital to commemorate the centenary of their independence from Spain. Valle-Inclán accepted with alacrity and travelled there via New York and Havana. Naturally enough, he was not idle during his stay, and apart from literary activities he succeeded in alienating the Spanish landowners by declaring in public that he favored the distribution of the land to the peasants and the setting up of the *ejido* system of agriculture. His undoubtedly sincere sympathy for the Mexican Indian was to be expressed in his novelistic masterpiece *Tirano Banderas (The Tyrant)*, 1926, which was inspired by his second visit to Mexico.

In the 1920's the author's powers of invention reached their highest point, and works of a high caliber followed one another in rapid succession. The year 1920 saw the publication of two plays with contrasting settings: *Divinas palabras (Divine Words)*, set in rural Galicia, and *Luces de bohemia (Bohemian Lights)*, whose background is Madrid in 1920. In the same year the author published a farce whose mood is much more frivolous than that of either play just mentioned. The work in question is *Farsa y licencia de la reina castiza (The Farce of the Castilian Queen)*, whose subject matter reveals that Valle's interest has shifted from Carlist to "official" Spain. In 1921 the magazine *La Pluma* serialized what was to prove Valle's finest *esperpento* in dramatic form, *Los cuernos de don Friolera (Don Friolera's Horns)*. But, just to show how many facets there were to his talent, he turned from this to *Cara de plata (Silver Face)*, 1922, thus completing the trilogy *Comedias bárbaras (The Vandals)*, started so many years before.

In 1923 the author's health, which had been uncertain for a long time, took a turn for the worse and he underwent surgery at a clinic in Santiago de Compostela. After his recovery Valle decided to return to Madrid with his family and the move was made a few months later. Two macabre one-act plays written in a savagely humorous vein appeared in the following year, 1924. One of these, *La cabeza del bautista (The Baptist's Head)*, was performed together with the earlier *modernista Cuento de abril (April Story)* at the Teatro del Centro in Madrid. The former was also staged in Barcelona in 1925. Now at the peak of his success as a writer, Valle-Inclán's activities embraced not only creative writing but also the dissemination of literature through lectures and, as an authoritative voice among Spanish men of letters, he attacked the régime of Primo de Rivera. Exasperated by Valle's opposition to his government, Primo once referred to him as "that superlative writer but extravagant citizen."

The year 1926 saw a further series of interesting publications. Sections of the novel *The Tyrant* had begun to appear a year before in a magazine called *El estudiante*. The last of these, *Zacarías el cruzado (Zacharias the Scarred)*, was published as a story in its own right shortly before the novel itself. *Ecos de Asmodeo (Echoes from Asmodeo)*, another section from a future novel, also appeared on its own in 1926. This short story was to become the second section of *La corte de los milagros (The Court of Miracles)*, the first of an ambitious cycle of historical novels. The author's habit of publishing fragments of ambitious works in advance—Valle's life-long practice—is very helpful when tracing the development of his novelistic masterpieces. The last publication of 1926 that deserves mention is *El terno del difunto (The Dead Man's Suit)*, whose title was later changed to *Las galas del difunto (The Dead Man's Finery)*. It is one of the three *esperpentos* published in 1930 under the general title of *Martes de carnaval (Carnival Warriors* or *Shrove Tuesday)*.

Valle-Inclán's renewed interest in the stage was reflected not only in his production but also by his participation in the amateur theatrical group organized by the Baroja brothers which they had christened *The White Lark*. It was here that Valle's excellent one-act play *Ligazón (The Blood Pact)* received its première. The author was to form his own theater group, *The Cracked Pitcher*, a few months later.

Of the works published in 1927, by far the most significant is the novel to which I have already referred, *The Court of Miracles*. However, the most notorious was to prove *La hija del capitán (The Captain's daughter)*, an *esperpento* of inferior quality. In this play Valle provides his own scathing comment on certain political events of the hour and rails against the corruption of the military. The police were instructed to remove the offending *esperpento* from Madrid bookshops, and it cannot be said that the reading public lost much thereby. This was not to be his only clash with the authorities since in the same year he was arrested—though soon released—for creating a public disturbance at the première of a play which did not meet with his approval.

In 1929 Valle-Inclán was jailed for a fortnight on the trivial grounds that he had failed to pay a fine of 250 pesetas imposed on him for causing a further public disturbance, this time at the Palacio de la Música.

After the fall from power of Primo de Rivera, Valle made a second bid to win a seat in the Constituent Cortes. This time he stood, not for the Traditionalists, but for one of the many parties with radical programs formed after the end of the dictatorship. The district for which he stood was Corunna. But Valle-Inclán's newly acquired radicalism brought him no more success than his earlier intransigent conservatism. No doubt the Spanish parliament thereby lost a colorful and lively personality, but it is unlikely that the writer who was not known for his patience, tact, or ability to compromise, was the stuff of which successful politicians are made.

The year 1932 was to prove one of upheaval in terms of his private life. Domestic trouble led to his separation from his wife, after which he moved with the children to an old house in the Plaza de Congreso in a rather shabby district of Madrid. The author also had to face a grave economic setback because of the bankruptcy of his publishers, the Compañía Ibero-Americana de Publicaciones. Due to this financial reversal he began to contribute once again to newspapers, something he sought to avoid since he felt it had a detrimental effect on an author's style.[20] The newspaper *El Sol* started to serialize the third and last novel of his projected historical cycle in 1932. Unfortunately, Valle did not live to complete this novel, and it was only published in book form many years later.[21] An interesting addition to *The Court of Miracles,* which would appear to be an introduction to the entire cycle, also appeared in *El Sol* in 1932. In the same year he became seriously ill once more due to a recurrence of his old complaint. So grave was his condition deemed that a reporter slipped five pesetas to the caretaker of the building where he lived on the understanding that he should be the first to be informed of the writer's death. This incident fired Valle to write a bitter poem called "Testamento" ("My Will") of which there are numerous versions.

As a result of ill health, the last few years of the writer's life were not of intense creative activity, although the few fragments dating from this period are by no means bereft of interest. A series of articles published in the Madrid newspaper *Ahora* in 1933 and 1935 under the heading of *Correo diplomático (The Diplomatic Bag)* reveals a close knowledge of historical events he also glosses in the *Ruedo ibérico (Iberian Ring)* cycle. Also of interest is a fragment for a future novel of the same historical cycle called *El trueno dorado (Gilded Youth)*, which was serialized posthumously in *Ahora* (1936).

In 1933, while still convalescing at the clinic where he had undergone surgery, Valle was told that he had been given an official post in Rome by the Republican government. This action was taken in the light of his very reduced economic circumstances. He travelled to Rome to take up the directorship of the Spanish Academy of Fine Arts, but realized after a short while that the task was beyond him since the improvement in his health was to prove illusory. Valle left Italy in the autumn when his health took a sudden turn for the worse and it was becoming patent to him that he could no longer keep up the pretence of carrying out administrative duties. Thus he returned to his native province in 1935 and was readmitted into the clinic of Doctor Iglesias. Here he died in 1936. Valle refused to have a priest at his bedside or to be given the Last Sacrament. He requested in advance that the burial service should not be a religious one. Given this implicit opposition to the Roman Catholic Church, coupled with the radical political tendencies of his later years, it may be said that he died at a judicious moment. Had he lived a few months longer Valle, like his great contemporary Unamuno, might have died under house arrest, or ended like García Lorca in an unknown grave, or been obliged to make the sad journey into exile undertaken by so many other Spanish writers. As it is, he was spared the grief of witnessing the holocaust he had predicted when in naming a collection of *esperpentos Shrove Tuesday* he had implied the imminence and the bleakness of Ash Wednesday.

CHAPTER 2

The Development of Valle-Inclán's Esthetic

IT is a striking and unusual feature of Valle-Inclán's works that in them he appears to reverse the usual artistic evolution from youth to old age. For it was in the novels and plays written in the 1920's—when he was approaching sixty—that he not only attained his full stature as a writer, but appeared most dynamic and inventive. It is now pertinent to analyze the reasons for this reversal of the normal process by a consideration of its cause and, in particular, of some of the major artistic movements which helped to mold Valle-Inclán's esthetics. Before we examine these in detail, it should be noted that Valle was to prove very sensitive to and even dependent on trends in the arts, as much during his formative period as a writer as later in life. Furthermore, he preferred to obtain his raw material, so to speak, from a foreign source rather than to rely on his own imagination for it.[1] This accounts for the charge often levelled at him that he plagiarized other writers' works without compunction. It should also be borne in mind, as I have already noted, that in general Valle was not prepared to indulge in serious study of this or that artistic movement, philosophical current or historical theory.[2] But what he did possess were very sensitive antennae which enabled him, as one critic has phrased it, "to intuit what was happening and to tune into the wave length of his period."[3] Thus it is possible both in his earlier and his later works to detect how current movements in the arts affected his production.

It is absolutely essential to the understanding of the personal philosophy evolved by Valle-Inclán and, consequently, of his esthetics, to relate his own doctrines to those of the Symbolists from whom they were culled at quite an early date. It is necessary also to see Valle-Inclán's work in the context of *Modernismo*, for one suspects that it was often through the leader of this

movement, Rubén Darío, that Valle acquired his knowledge
of the various trends evident at that time in French literature.

Personally, I would distinguish between two types of stimuli
which affect Valle-Inclán in different ways: the first of these
stems more directly from the *modernista* movement and affects
the author only temporarily and superficially. It accounts for
certain characteristics evident in both the style and content of
his earlier works up to around 1905. The second of these stimuli,
more long-lasting and fundamental in its impact, mystical in
quality, was to affect all his mature production and is owed almost
exclusively to a particular approach to art which forms the her-
itage of Symbolism. Of course, it must be emphasized that the
two movements are by no means mutually exclusive; on the
contrary, the *modernistas* who were nothing if not eclectics, are
indebted to Symbolism as they are to other artistic movements.
For this reason it is not my intention to divide the two movements into rigid and arbitrary categories; however, more attention
will be devoted to Symbolism because not only was its impact on
Valle infinitely more decisive, but also because critics have paid
far more attention to *Modernismo*. Whereas the appeal of much
that is central to *Modernismo* wears off quite rapidly, the Symbolists' outlook on language and the material world is implicit
in those works in which Valle-Inclán reaches his full stature as
a writer.

I *Symbolism*

In her most illuminating study of Rimbaud, Enid Starkie notes
that esoteric cults holding out the promise to the initiate of
some form of superior revelation flourish when the power of
the Church is temporarily weakened.[4] Certainly, this theory can
be applied successfully to France in the nineteenth century,
where a current of mysticism began to manifest itself as from
the 1820's. It is apparent in at least two of Balzac's novels,
Séraphita and *Louis Lambert;* the attitude to poetry developed
by Victor Hugo in his later years is colored by it also.[5] Thereafter
this tendency gains momentum with the theosophy of Baudelaire
and, placed only temporarily in abeyance by the philosophy of
Positivism, emerges triumphant towards the end of the century
with the formulation of Symbolist doctrines and, on a more popular level, with the great vogue of spiritualism and the occult

sciences. I should like to consider this very important mystical current under two headings which reflect their major characteristics and explain their relevance in this period.

The creative artist who is repelled by the theories of Realists and Naturalists finds himself involved in a quest after two things. The first of these is a superior, transcendental world, the world of essences or the noumenon. This is contrasted with the natural world of phenomena rejected by the artist because it is mutable and relative. The second is a desire for unity, synthesis or harmony in the world of the senses: a feeling that man should not look on nature as being divided into a mass of heterogeneous phenomena in which no single unit bears any obvious relation to the others, but, rather, as having a close affinity and partaking of the self-same identity. In effect, the two aspects of this search overlap, since the desire for a coherent order and unity in the material world reflects, on a lower plane, the same quest of the Absolute in a transcendental sphere. For some understanding—albeit only partial—of how this attitude came into prominence in France, it is necessary to consider firstly the influence of Schopenhauer, Baudelaire and Richard Wagner; secondly that of Pythagoras and the Gnostics, since in both cases Valle was attracted by the esoteric elements in their doctrines.

1. *Schopenhauer*

Schopenhauer's philosophy—or the somewhat distorted view of it held by the writers we are to consider—had a considerable impact in France which became more pronounced as from the early 1870's. This was partly owed to the fact that its pessimistic message harmonized with the mood of disillusionment evident in France in the early years of the Third Republic. A further reason was a study of Schopenhauer published by Ribot in 1874. Téodor de Wyzewa, a leading exegete and critic of the Symbolist movement, recommended the study of the German philosopher to all prospective Idealists. This is because their reaction to his philosophy was similar to that of Baudelaire's after the latter's introduction to Poe: the views expressed tended to confirm their own ideas.

According to Schopenhauer, men are the playthings of a blind Will to which every living creature is utterly subservient. The only purpose of this Will which dominates the material world is to ensure the continuation of the race, hence its seat is in the reproductive organs. This Will is blind, destructive and utterly egocentric. There are but two ways of escape from it: one is fallible and temporary; the second complete and final. It is with the first that we are concerned, since it was this one which was likely to appeal to the artists under consideration.

Schopenhauer maintains that the individual can find temporary liberation from the thraldom of Will in art. In the objective contemplation of Beauty he loses his personality and becomes "pure knowing subject." In this way the victim of Will is temporarily freed and the esthetic delight annuls those pleasures and pains which result from the workings of the Will. Art is the state of the most complete mental objectivity; consequently while involved in its contemplation the human being loses consciousness of his individuality; individuality is, after all, only an illusion. Once freed from the clutches of Will, man is able to love and to feel compassion for his fellow creatures, conscious now of their plight which he shares. But, as long as he is dominated by Will, he feels only hostility towards others for, as has already been noted, the Will is completely egoistic. Schopenhauer's philosophy is derived to some extent from Plato's in that he avails himself of the latter's concept of Forms or Ideas. These Forms are the quintessence or the ideal in the superior world of every natural phenomenon in the imperfect world we inhabit.

The philosophy of Schopenhauer appealed to the artist of this period, that is, of the 1870's and 1880's, in two ways. Firstly, it raised the status of art to a very high level indeed and rid it of any utilitarian purpose.[6] Secondly, it introduced him to Plato's theory of Forms, thus confirming his disenchantment with the external world and giving him fresh impetus to reach the "real" world of essences through his art.

2. *Baudelaire*

Baudelaire's particular contribution to the development of these mystical and metaphysical currents was the doctrine of universal analogies or correspondences expressed in the famous sonnet "Correspondances."[7] In point of fact, the idea of the universal analogy was not of Baudelaire's invention as he himself was the first to admit.[8] The concept stems from the eighteenth-century mystic Swedenborg, while certain of Baudelaire's contemporaries such as Toussenel and Fourier also played a prominent part in the formulation of his theories on the subject.[9] However, when all is said and done, there can be no question that but for Baudelaire the concept of universal analogies would have been forgotten long ago. To him must go the credit for both perfecting and popularizing it.

Briefly, Baudelaire's idea was the following: there is in all aspects of creation a profound unity; all living things have a dual nature which is partly material and partly spiritual. There exists between the celestial and the physical realms a link or correspondence whereby everything on the terrestrial plane has its equivalent—of which it is but a pale shadow—in the spiritual world. There is also another form of correspondence between different phenomena in the physical world and, particularly, between the senses. This type of correspondence is usually termed synaesthesia. According to Baudelaire there are distinct cross-references between the senses, so that a sound may be equated with a scent or smell, the visual related to the tactile, etc. . . . Furthermore, such correspondences need not be limited to the senses. For example, the color violet conjures up for Baudelaire "a love that is contained, veiled and mysterious."[10]

Thus, as Jean Pommier points out in his absorbing study of Baudelaire's mysticism, the idea of correspondences exists on two distinct levels: one involving depth and the other breadth. The one of deeper significance is that of the universal analogy, stemming from Swedenborg, which associates every living thing with an equivalent in the transcendental sphere. The second level involves breadth rather than depth in that it reveals the underlying relationship of phenomena on the terrestrial plane. Baudelaire's mystical vision of the universe and its poetic significance is summarized by Enid Starkie in the following way:

"His esthetic doctrine is closely linked with his spiritual convictions and he cannot understand the one without realizing the other. He believed, to express it in Swedenborgian language, that all things in the material world were a correspondence of things in the spiritual world, that they were the imperfect images of heavenly beauty . . . it is not possible for us to see the objects in the spiritual world except indirectly through their symbols. These symbols are the language of nature, a hieroglyphic language spread before us unread, or else only imperfectly read. . . .

Baudelaire was convinced that only artists who had reached a high state of spirituality would be successful in discovering images, metaphors and analogies for the adequate rendering of their vision. He believed that genius lay not in the power of invention, but in the faculty of reception. The artist can be no more than a translator . . ."[11]

What emerges very clearly from Baudelaire's conception of the universe and the interplay of spirit and matter on which it is posited, is an urgent need for harmony and unity. For this reason it is not surprising that Baudelaire should have aspired after a synthesis of all the arts; a fusion of the senses into one supreme expression of beauty. It is precisely this idea which drew him to the esthetic and the music of Richard Wagner.

3. *Richard Wagner*

Baudelaire, like the Symbolists after him, regarded music as the supreme art form owing primarily to its subtlety: music, unlike words, is not concerned with direct statements. It implies, suggests, moving the spirit of the listener and creating a state of mind rather than communicating a concrete thought or sensation. However, this alone is not enough to account for the Symbolists' admiration of Wagner since it only explains their predilection for music in general.[12] It is possible to adduce more specific reasons.

Wagner himself believed in the supremacy of music over the other arts,[13] the reason being that music, unlike painting or narrative, knows no frontiers. Consequently music tends to eliminate what Mallarmé terms "the contingent" *(le hasard)* and moves in the sphere of essences. Because of its evident superiority, music can never stand alone. That which is the embodiment of inner feelings must be associated with one of the more lowly arts so as to be fully comprehensible. In fact it should be associated preferably with all of them. Thus what Wagner deemed the finest vehicle for a total art was a music drama involving the interplay of poetry, mime, décor and music.

Another feature of Wagner's esthetic that appealed to Baudelaire, in that it confirmed his own views, was the use of symbolism in Wagnerian operas. In *Tannhäuser,* for example, Wagner is concerned with the material expression of the gulf separating the body and the soul; Heaven and Hell. Through these symbols and the fusion of the arts into a total art, Wagner sought to raise his audience from the world in which everything is relative and mutable to that of the Absolute.

Thus the Symbolists agreed with Wagner's assertion that music is a supremely important element in art, in that it is the least imperfect instrument for bringing the individual into touch with the world of essences. So it became their avowed intent to wrest back from music what poetry had lost to it, and to bring poetry as close as possible to music by using words for their melodic and symbolic content rather than their intellectual meaning. In this way words assume a magic significance; they are destined to induce a state of trance in the listener which will conjure up the unheard music, the vision of the Absolute: "To express the idea with the help of words, to suggest emotions by the music of these words, such is, in my view, the Alpha and Omega of our doctrine."[14]

II *Pythagorean Metaphysics and Gnosticism*

1. *Pythagoras*

As Guy Michaud indicates in the introduction to his *La Doctrine symboliste (Documents)*, one is advised to speak of a doctrine rather than of a variety of poetic theories when considering the Symbolist movement. Theirs is an attempt, Michaud declares, to return to traditional metaphysics, to the beliefs at the heart of all ancient philosophies and great religions. Intent on grasping the essence of poetry, the Symbolists were led into an investigation of the essence of the universe so as to understand the significance and the sense of poetic creation. This accounts for the attraction they felt for the mysteries of ancient religions and, in consequence, the relevance of Pythagoras and Gnosticism in this context.

In 1889 a member of the Symbolist movement, Edouard Schuré, published a study of the esoteric content of certain great religions and metaphysical doctrines. Its purpose was to indicate their underlying unity. Schuré's thesis is that while the more superficial aspects of various beliefs, namely their ritual and dogma, may show marked differences, their conception of the universe and of man's relation to the superior world is fundamentally the same: "The essential principles of esoteric doctrine may be formulated as follows: Spirit is the only reality. Matter is nothing but its lower, changing, ephemeral expression, its dynamism in space and time."[15] It would be superfluous to explain why such a conclusion would be likely to appeal to an adherent of Symbolism and to increase his interest in esoteric sciences. In Schuré's work a lengthy section is devoted to Pythagoras and, since Valle-Inclán was to reveal a pronounced interest in certain aspects of Pythagorean metaphysics, it is worth examining its complexities so that the knowledge can be applied later to the structure of the author's novels. The summary I now give is based on Schuré's study because it is very likely that this was Valle's source.

Pythagoras evolved a numerical explanation of the universe, posited on the triple nature of both man and the macrocosm. According to him, man is composed of three elements, body, soul, and spirit. These divisions are reflected in nature which is divided into three concentric spheres, the natural, the human, and the divine. Man and Nature are crowned by the divine unity which is itself a trinity. The keys of the universe are contained in Number and Music. According to Pythagoras "Numbers . . . contain the secret of things and God is universal harmony."[16]

Aristotle dwells rather laconically on Pythagoras' theory of Numbers in his *Metaphysics,* pointing out that to Pythagoras and his followers the principles of mathematics were the principle of all things. Aristotle then continues:

"Since of these principles numbers are by nature the first, and in number they [Pythagoras and his followers] seemed to see many resemblances to the things that exist and come into being—more than in fire, earth and water—since, again, they saw that the modifications and ratios of the musical scales were expressible in numbers; since, then, all other things seemed in their whole nature to be modeled on numbers, and numbers seemed to be the first thing in the whole of nature, they supposed the elements of number to be the element of all things, and the whole heaven to be a musical scale and a number. And all the properties of numbers and scales which they could show to agree with the attributes and parts and the whole arrangement of the heavens, they collected and fitted into their scheme; and if there was

a gap anywhere, they readily made additions so as to make their
whole theory coherent."[17]

In addition, Pythagoras maintained that there is a ternary law
regulating human beings and a septenary law governing their
evolution. To seven is granted the distinction of absolute isolation
and first cousinage to the Monad or Essence which is expressed
by One. Seven is the universal number because of the innumer-
able heptads in the microcosm and macrocosm, such as the seven
gates of the body, the seven planets, the seven days of the week,
and the seven colors of light. Three is a magical number too
because, as I have already mentioned, man is composed of three
elements which are distinct though blended in one another.
These three elements have equivalents in the universe with its
three concentric spheres, the natural, the human, and the divine
world. This ternary law is by no means limited to Pythagoras
alone; it is, rather, a cornerstone of esoteric science. Pythagoras
believed it was encountered at every step on the ladder of life,
revealing the inner structure of the universe, showing the infinite
correspondences of the microcosm and the macrocosm.

Pythagoras called his disciples mathematicians, but the science
of Number was at once beyond the sphere of human experience
even though more relevant to man's condition than orthodox
mathematics. Number was not regarded as an abstract quantity
but as the intrinsic and active virtue of God, the source of universal harmony. Each number contained a principle, a law, an
active force of the universe. Thus seven, the compound of three
and four, signifies the union of man and divinity,[18] while ten,
formed by the addition of the first four numbers and containing
them all, is the perfect number, for it represents all the principles
of divinity evolved and reunited in a new unity.

There remain two other aspects of Pythagoras' thought which
find an echo in the work Valle-Inclán devoted to his esthetic,
namely La lámpara maravillosa (The Wonderful Lamp); although
unlike the science of Numbers they do not find obvious expression
in the rest of Valle's production. The first of these aspects is
the significance attributed to light, which is shared by the adepts
of Cabala.[19] Schuré remarks that from the beginning of civilization the worship of Aryan humanity was directed towards the
sun as the source of light, heat and life. He then continues:

When the thought of the sages rose from the phenomenon to the cause, they formed the concept of an immaterial fire, an intelligible light. . . . The astral light is revealed as the universal medium of the phenomena of vision and of ecstacy. . . . Once transported into this element, the spirit of the seer leaves corporeal conditions. For him opaque matter becomes transparent, and the soul, disengaging itself from the body and rising in its own light, penetrates in a state of ecstasy into the spiritual world . . .[20]

The sun is the emblem of the union between the world of matter and that of the spirit. It is the way for the visionary to approach the source of Divine love and to discard in the process the illusion of individuality which otherwise impedes such union.

The last point which is relevant in the context of Valle-Inclán is Pythagoras' belief that all matter is sensible and possesses a soul. This is linked with the doctrine of metempsychosis whereby eternity is only attained by the spirit after a long pilgrimage through a succession of lives, thus undergoing a process of purification: as one life succeeds another, the spirit should find itself ever higher up the ladder of existence. This is because of the recollection of previous lives which helps it to attain its goal of eternal rest.

Such an esoteric science was bound to appeal to the Symbolists for more than one reason. Firstly, it should be remembered that mystery and obscurity were cultivated by the followers of this movement. Pythagoras' doctrine is sibylline; it required initiation for its meaning to be clarified. Secondly, it stressed the unity and harmony of the universe and the essential correspondence between man, nature, and the transcendental world. Thirdly, Pythagoras used numbers symbolically: three, seven and the remaining primary numbers are not mere digits: they are magical numbers on which rests an entire metaphysical structure.

2.   Gnosticism

As with Pythagorean metaphysics, it is not necessary for the purposes of this study to give a detailed account of the various Gnostic or Gnosticist[21] sects and their doctrines. Valle-Inclán exercised a certain discrimination in his borrowings, alighting on points that interested him in the works of a variety of religious and philosophic thinkers, fusing them subsequently into a harmonious whole. With regard to the Gnostics, Valle is indebted to them for two concepts of fundamental importance in his work. The first of these is that only the base world of the senses is condemned to cyclical time; the second is that all matter is inherently evil.

The Gnostic sects were active in the first six centuries of the Christian era, reaching their full flowering in the second and third centuries A.D. The movement appears to have started in Syria, spreading later to other parts of Southeast Asia and to North Africa. Naturally enough, there are differences to be observed in the beliefs of the various sects loosely grouped together as Gnostic, but these do not apply to the fundamental points which are our concern at present.

Central to Gnostic myths, whether they be simple or extremely elaborate, is the idea of a Fall from the Pleroma (Plenitude) which in all cases is the result of sin or weakness; for example, arrogance or a disordered passion. Thus, what was formerly an eon or emanation abiding in the Totality or All, finds itself condemned to regions of darkness. Furthermore, it is prevented from re-entering the Pleroma by the Horus (Limit).[22] In the case of more than one Gnostic myth, the guilty eon is Sophia (Wisdom) who, in her arrogance, thinks that like the Unnameable Abyss and his consort Nous or Thought—the first pair of eons—she can conceive without being fertilized. Sophia is punished by giving birth to a misshapen substance. This is the Demiurge, responsible for the creation of the visible worlds and the Earth.

The Gnostic attitude toward time is the direct result of the sect's view of the world and the myths in which this view finds its allegorical expression. The base world of the senses (unlike the Pleroma which is timeless) is the province of cyclical time, and Fatality is inherent in it. It follows that because time is considered cyclical, events on Earth will recur at set intervals. Thus the Gnostic view of time is diametrically opposed to that of the Christians for whom time is rectilinear, unfolding uninterruptedly from Creation towards Judgment Day.

Because the material world was created by the Demiurge, the product of his mother's sin, it is condemned as evil and the Pleroma is foreign to it. The power ruling over the cosmos is weak, ignorant, and perverse. Redemption for the Gnostic is not to be found in love, faith or deeds, but in knowledge. He must become an adept to gain possession of the saving knowledge. For this reason, as Victor White indicates,[23] there is in Gnosticism a twofold dualism: firstly of mankind—in that only the few who have mastered the esoteric lore can aspire to salvation; secondly, there is a dualism in the philosophic sense, for there is no link at all between the Pleroma or Totality and the world of matter, by its very nature hostile and chaotic.

Thus, unlike Pythagoras' or Baudelaire's vision of the universe, there is in Gnostic beliefs no idea of harmony or of a relationship between the celestial and material spheres. Gnosticism is by its very nature aristocratic and exclusive, since it is only the elect with knowledge or *gnosis* to whom salvation is held out. This aristocratic bias had an obvious attraction for members of the Symbolist movement who raised poetry to a quasi-religious level which only the privileged could hope to grasp. This is made abundantly clear by Mallarmé: "Poetry is the expression, through human language reduced to its essential rhythm, of the mysterious sense of existence in its various manifestations: thus it grants authenticity to our stay on earth *and constitutes the sole spiritual task.*"[24]

III   Modernismo

Modernismo arose in Latin America, its acknowledged leader being the Nicaraguan poet Rubén Darío. It was initially a movement of esthetic renewal, revolutionary in artistic terms alone, although later it was to acquire political overtones: pride in the continent's pre-Columbian civilizations and defiance of their Anglo-Saxon "Big Brother" to the North. So far as Valle is concerned, it is unnecessary to consider the later development of the movement.

Modernismo—in common with Symbolism—is a revolt against the commonplace, mundane, and vulgar. The artist, distressed by a society which he finds personally distasteful, refuses commitment and takes refuge in an exquisite, artificial world of his own devising. The rider to this artistic bias—one of the most pronounced features of the movement—is disdain for that favorite whipping boy of the nineteenth-century writer, the "bon bourgeois" whom the *modernista* loves to shock or *epatar* according to the gallicism used at the time to express this point.[25] *Mod-*

ernistas tend to lean rather heavily on cultural props. Their works, be they poetry or prose, are enhanced by copious allusions to statuary and *bibelots* from exotic places, to the artistic refinements of France in the eighteenth century and to the myths and culture of ancient Greece. The attraction felt for the Greek myths is significant in that this is poetry of a pagan, sensual nature.[26] There is little appeal to the intellect or the spirit in *modernista* works; their province, by choice, is the senses. Their ideal is *lo bello* rather than *lo Hermoso*. In other words what appears beautiful to the senses rather than to the spirit.

Coupled with the innovations in terms of content was one of style. The need was felt in the Hispano-American world in the last decades of the nineteenth century to renew the very stuff of the language after the pummeling it had received at the hands of grandiloquent Romantics such as the Duque de Rivas or Zorrilla and the pedestrian poets of the next generation. To this end, the *modernistas* turned to France for inspiration and the reinvigoration of their own poetry. They borrowed freely—though not always with discernment—from Hugo, the Parnassian poets, and the Symbolists. Thus their credo is a somewhat makeshift and hybrid affair, more of a mosaic than a well-defined and consistent set of ideas on art.[27]

Such features as their aristocratic outlook and the escapist nature of their works are, of course, inherited from certain of the Romantics. Another legacy of this movement is the *modernistas'* fondness for strong sensations. In *The Decline and Fall of the Romantic Ideal*,[28] F. L. Lucas explains how and why this emphasis arose. According to him, the writer's palate grew progressively more jaded during the course of the nineteenth century, so that sensations had to be made ever more violent. With the passage of time they degenerated into the cult of the morbid, the erotically perverse, the sadistic and the diabolic. These features, as I shall show later, are much in evidence in the major *modernista* works of Valle-Inclán.

Despite their undoubted debt to the Romantics, the *modernistas* also borrowed certain of their ideas and techniques from the Symbolists. However, it should be added that the metaphysical preoccupations of the French writers are less pronounced in *modernista* verse. The *modernistas* laid much emphasis on the musical value of words in poetry as well as prose, the intention being, in the case of the latter, to provide short, melodious and well-balanced periods while at the same time revitalizing the language by the introduction of archaisms, neologisms and foreign terms. The *modernistas* were also interested in Baudelaire's theory of correspondences, though they tended to concentrate on the affinities of physical phenomena rather than on the transcendental aspects of the universal analogy. All these ideas were to color the poetry of Darío and, through him, that of other Latin-American poets and, in time, those of the peninsula too.

One last and very important point must be made, namely that the hallmark of the period is the cult of the artificial. The figure who epitomizes this cult is the hero of Huysmans' novel *A Rebours*. This character, Des Esseintes, was determined to subject nature to art to such an extent that by selection and cross-breeding he evolved bizarre hybrid blooms which looked utterly counterfeit. The artist's scorn for nature is fittingly summarized in Wilde's dictum: "Art is our spirited protest, our gallant attempt to teach Nature her proper place."[29] Years after he had abandoned the *modernista* credo, Valle-Inclán was to describe his most famous works of that period as "literature fashioned from literature." In this way he acknowledged that these were indeed period pieces bearing the stamp of the outstanding *fin de siècle* writers to whom he and his fellow *modernistas* owed so pronounced a debt.

There remains as yet to determine how exactly Valle came into contact with Rubén Darío when the former's artistic tastes were still comparatively unformed. The Nicaraguan poet paid his first visit to Spain in 1892, but at this time he was not yet very well known. His name was only to become established four years later with the publication in Buenos Aires of a verse collection entitled *Prosas profanas*. Six years after his first visit to the Peninsula, Rubén Darío returned to Madrid as a correspondent for the Argentine newspaper *La Nación*. On this occasion his reception was triumphal: aspiring writers lionized him, since the novelty of his verse was precisely what was required to fill the vacuum left by pompous, rhetorical rhymesters of the previous generation such as Campoamor and Núñez de Arce.

In point of fact, Valle-Inclán must have come into contact with Darío's work before 1898, or at least this is the impression derived from the short stories of *Femeninas (Feminine Cameos)*. This is indeed quite likely since Darío's first collection of verse and prose, which bore the then fashionable title of *Azul (Azure)*, was published in 1888. At the same time, since Darío acted in part as a disseminator in the Hispanic world of contemporary French literature, it is equally likely that the *modernista* features in *Femeninas* stem directly from French sources without Darío acting as intermediary.[30]

Although this is a controversial viewpoint, it is my opinion that the *modernista* esthetic exercised a regrettable influence on Valle's works, because its tenets and assumptions ran contrary to his own talents. So much superimposed *collage* and so much foreign material acted as a straitjacket and inhibited his talents until he discarded them, for they were artificial and alien to his temperament. However, Valle owed one great debt to the movement, as did many writers of his generation and the following one: the effect of *Modernismo* on the Spanish language was altogether striking. Both in prose and poetry—and in some cases the dividing line was rendered deliberately vague—the language became more graceful, polished and subtle. In this one sense Valle remained an avowed *modernista* in the *esperpento* period which will shortly be discussed.

IV   La lámpara maravillosa

By way of conclusion to the first part of this chapter, I should like to indicate the resemblances between Valle-Inclán's esthetic as outlined in *La lámpara maravillosa (The Wonderful Lamp)* and that of the Symbolists. An analysis of the *modernista* aspects of his earlier works will be given in the next chapter when these are considered in some detail. But since the debt to the Symbolists is at once more diffused in his output and more fundamental to it, it is wiser to establish any comparisons between Symbolism and his own work that are tenable before embarking on a more detailed study of Valle-Inclán's production.

The Wonderful Lamp, whose subtitle is "Spiritual Exercises," was first published in 1916, although written three years earlier. It is a work whose significance was only barely appreciated by scholars and critics until quite recently. At least one reason for the earlier curt dismissal of this work is that at first glance it can appear somewhat impenetrable. Unless the reader is

familiar with the philosophic and esoteric doctrines on which
the writer is drawing, its significance may well elude him.
Consequently the tendency was to ignore it and describe it
casually as a meandering and deliberately obscure work. The
witticism attributed to Valle-Inclán's contemporary, the poet
Juan Ramón Jiménez, typifies this attitude: "The trouble with
Valle's lamp," he quipped, "is that it contains no oil—only
smoke."[31] The remark may still be considered droll; it can no
longer be accepted as just. *The Wonderful Lamp* is in fact the
key to Valle-Inclán's work. Without this key he can only be
considered a brilliant stylist, for the reader remains unaware of
the philosophy underlying his work which, once known, lends
new meaning to the whole.

Valle-Inclán begins his "spiritual exercises" by saying that
there are two ways of acquiring knowledge: one is the search
after truth by rational means, that is, by a process of gradual
enlightenment; the other is by irrational, intuitive methods. The
second, as one might expect, is the one favored by Valle-Inclán,
for it leads to absolute knowledge and brings quietude in its
wake. To this end it is necessary to undergo a rigorous initiation,
similar to that of the mystic in his search for the ecstacy of union
with the godhead.[32] This, in translation, is how Valle expresses
the point: "The poet like the mystic must perceive what lies
beyond the limit imposed by the senses, so as to glimpse through
the fiction of the moment and the seeming passage of the hours
the labor of eternity."[33] The thought underlying this work which
gives it unity is the need for release from the world of matter.
Both art and religious experience are ways towards it.

The passage quoted above with its reference to the error of
time serves as an indication of Valle-Inclán's Gnosticist leanings.
In *The Wonderful Lamp* there are frequent allusions to Gnostic
beliefs. As already indicated, they refer in the main to time
and the need to rise above the flesh—which is evil—by initiation
into the esoteric sciences. At one point the writer dwells on the
attainment of total beauty and the period of travail which preceded it: "Before I felt union with Beauty and its accompanying
repose—divine ecstasy—I experienced a sense of futility and
anguish due to my awareness of movement and the sterile nature
of life. That Spirit constantly erasing its tracks had me in thrall
and my existence was like a mocking echo of its flight in the

Horus of the Pleroma."[34] Throughout this work there are numerous references to the circle which symbolizes two distinct and
contradictory things. It sometimes represents the cyclical time of
man and the limit beyond which lies Totality,[35] but may also
refer to the entry of the soul into the Pleroma and moments of
fulfilment and quietude.[36]

Although the doctrines incorporated in this text are of fundamental importance in the formulation of Valle's esthetic, also
visible in *The Wonderful Lamp*, as I have already indicated,
are borrowings from other esoteric beliefs and philosophies. The
work is in fact an amalgam of various doctrines. There are
frequent allusions to the relationship binding all phenomena
in the material world;[37] to Pythagoras' concept of metempsychosis
whereby wisdom is defined as the collected memory of previous
existences;[38] to the theory of Number[39] and to the essential part
played by the sun in bringing the human being into touch with
the superior world.[40] In so far as philosophers are concerned,
Valle-Inclán is drawn by the Platonic doctrine of Forms. He
also devotes a long passage to glossing the basic principles underlying Schopenhauer's philosophy, namely Will as the moving
force of the universe.[41]

An extensive section of *The Wonderful Lamp* is devoted to
language. Here again the reader is conscious of the influence
exercised on Valle by the Symbolists. What the author stresses
above all else is the evocative power of words stemming from
their musical quality. Only by trusting in the melody of the word
can the poet hope to evoke what lies beyond the realm of the
senses: "He who at some point manages to break loose from
the prison of the senses can invest words with a new meaning
like a tunic of light. Then his language becomes sibylline."[42]
The esoteric significance which the poet in his rôle as seer is able
to lend to words is reiterated at a later point in the same chapter:
"The secret of human consciences can only be divulged through
the musical miracle of words. Thus the poet is closest to divinity
when he is most hermetic. The obscurities will not be deliberate
but will flow from the abyss of his emotions which separates him
from the world."[43]

However, it must be stressed that by no means everything in
the important section on language is derivative. Much of it is
dedicated to the development of language in Spain and to what

the author considers its three principal manifestations, Galician, Castilian and Catalan, each one representing the character of its people. The ideas set forth here are the result of personal reflection; the point made by Valle about Castilian is that the language is out of touch with the twentieth century. Castilian has remained as though petrified in its Golden Age form, no longer reflecting the spirit of the nation. The author feels that during Spain's period of greatness Castilian was consciously molded on Latin and that the result of this was "four centuries of vain and boastful literature."[44] What he is endeavoring to do is to "dig the pit where we may bury the hollow and grandiloquent prose of Castile."[45] Spain has no call to rehearse her gestures for the world because there is no longer an audience. Instead she must become inward-looking so as to fashion a warm and sincere mode of expression relevant to the age and the country's situation.

If the scope of this study permitted it, it would be possible to indicate a number of other features which relate Valle-Inclán's esthetic to Symbolism. However, the most significant aspects of *The Wonderful Lamp* have been mentioned and the outline given of Valle-Inclán's philosophy of art. These will be considered in Chapter Three in relation to his production.

V The Esperpento

In Valle-Inclán's writing career there are two periods of intense creativity separated by a gap when his output is, relatively speaking, meager and less inspired than either the earlier or later works. But this interim period is of crucial importance in that it gave the author a respite in which to take stock of his achievements, to rethink his approach to writing and to decide whether or not any fundamental change of direction was required. It is significant that *The Wonderful Lamp* belongs to this interim period, which represents a watershed in his literary career. In it he gives expression to his philosophy of art or, if one prefers, to art as a philosophy of life, reflected in his earlier works in *modernista* guise. What occurs subsequently is that the author rejects the outward forms of the esthetic while retaining those fundamental doctrines culled from the Symbolists and the esoteric writers to whom they themselves were drawn. Valle came to realize that the superficial aspects of *Modernismo* were outdated.

With this knowledge he begins to draw on the techniques of certain avant-garde movements in European literature such as Expressionism, Futurism and Cubism, combining these novel aspects which relate principally to the writer's craft with the ideas implicit in his earlier works. The latter are not discarded—only modified—in his later production.

It cannot be doubted that such anarchic movements as those mentioned above affected his work in some measure. But whereas in the case of Symbolism it is possible to establish detailed comparisons and to show how Symbolist doctrines affected his outlook on life, this is by no means the case with the later movements. It is true that the author himself will often hint at the attraction he felt for such movements as, for example, when he writes "Cubist vision of the Harris Circus." However, their presence in his work is best described as an unmistakable atmosphere or aura in which elements from a variety of sources have been fused into a harmonious whole after a process of rigorous selection.

There is more involved in the change from the earlier to the later works than loss of faith in the *modernista* credo. It is a fact that after a period of withdrawal, when the Symbolists chose to ignore the world around them, devoting their lives completely to art, there followed a period of almost inevitable reaction. This was due to a feeling of disquiet, a realization that the artist who can only communicate with a cultured élite is at least partly impotent and certainly not as effective as he might be. This state of mind was summed up by Paul Valéry in the last stanza of "Le cimetière marin" when he wrote "The wind is rising, we must attempt to live." In this context one should recall the famous remark made by Axel in Villiers de L'Isle Adam's *Le Château d'Axel (Axel's Castle)* some years before: "Live? I leave that to the servants."[46] Valle, as a follower of the Symbolist credo, had chosen to bury his head ostrich-like in the sand and to dispense with the world about him. Now, during this interregnum which roughly spans the years 1909-1917, he appears to conclude that it is time to devote his attention to the problems and evils of contemporary Spain. He will impose on himself the task of satirizing and castigating his country and its people for what are, in his opinion, very serious drawbacks. The bulk of Valle's satire is to be concentrated on socio-political matters.

It is evident from the bitterness with which Valle castigates his fellow-countrymen that his mood is one of profound disenchantment. The reasons for this are twofold. The first, which is probably the more important of the two, is the grimness of the political scene in the Spain of his period, with rigged elections, Anarchist-inspired proletarian uprisings, and an incompetent and corrupt army operating on a spoils system. Of course, Valle-Inclán was by no means the only writer of this period to experience a sense of disgust at the state of the body politic: vocal too in this respect were Antonio Machado, Unamuno and Baroja, although they differed from Valle-Inclán in that their trenchant criticisms of Spain started at a much earlier date. It is for this reason that a well-known critic, Pedro Salinas, has described Valle as "the prodigal son of the 1898 generation."[47]

The second possible reason for Valle-Inclán's disillusionment, with mankind in general rather than with his own countrymen, was the trauma resulting from a visit to the Western Front in France in the years 1916-1917. Although this is only a surmise, it would appear likely that this experience was decisive in changing his outlook on war. It will be seen later that in his more youthful works Valle had shown a keen interest in war and warriors, admiring the qualities and characteristics traditionally associated with the military. Valle-Inclán's knowledge of war had been gleaned in the main from the second Carlist War. This type of civil war, involving only small bodies of troops fighting in skirmishes rather than pitched battles could appear glamorous and exciting, particularly to someone who was emotionally very committed to the Carlist cause. Consequently, the vision of destruction, mutilation, disease, and abject misery on a scale far greater than man had ever known which faced the author in France, was bound to seem a grim and mocking retort to the earlier glorification of war expressed through his alter ego Xavier de Bradomín: "I too [like the Conquistadors of the sixteenth century] feel that horror is beautiful, and love the glorious purple of blood, and the sacking of villages, and the cruel veterans, those who violate maidens, burn crops, and all those who commit outrages when shielded by the military code."[48] How was any sensitive individual to reconcile this vain product of an imagination overstimulated by literary trends with what was in effect taking place? There was no way of harmonizing fantasy with reality, and the result was violent reaction coupled with profound depression and anger against the military for condoning such moral aberrations. It must also be borne in mind that Valle's now intense dislike of war and warriors was increased by the incompetence of the armed services in his own country at that time.

It is evident that the sum total of Valle-Inclán's experiences, observation, and meditations were bound to cause a radical redirection of his work. The author came to feel, furthermore, that his newfound esthetic required a personal instrument for its expression, a genre of his own devising. Thus he created the *esperpento*.

According to Valle-Inclán, there are three ways an author may regard the characters of his own invention. The first position he can assume is one of reverence, on his knees, regarding his creations with awe; the second is to place the character on the same level, looking him squarely in the face and regarding him as an equal; the third, and it is this one Valle feels is most typical of the Spanish writer, is to look down on the character from a height, assuming the position of a god who is indifferent to the petty squabbles of the human beings below him. It is the last of these positions Valle is to favor in the *esperpento* period.

Valle first formulated his new esthetic, expressing it in lucid terms, in a novel in dramatic form called *Luces de bohemia (Bohemian Lights)*. But in fact, as I shall indicate later, there are clear signs of an artistic and ideological reorientation in the earlier verse collection *La pipa de kif (The Marihuana Pipe)* and the play *Farsa y licencia de la reina castiza (Farce of the Castilian Queen)*. For the moment, however, it will suffice to limit the analysis of the *esperpento* to the now famous passage from *Luces de bohemia*. Two of the principal characters in the play are shuffling home after an all-night session in the cafés and taverns of Madrid. One of them is the protagonist, Max Estrella, a blind poet down on his luck owing to the incapacity of his countrymen to recognize or appreciate literary talent; the other is his faithful crony don Latino de Hispalís. At a certain point Max declares roundly that the true image of Spain can only be captured in a new literary form fashioned for this purpose. The passage in question is worth quoting at some length:

MAX: Our tragedy is not a tragedy at all.
DON LATINO: Well, it must be something!
MAX: The *Esperpento.*

. . . .

MAX: The *Ultraístas* are a bunch of charlatans.[49] *Esperpentismo* was invented by Goya. The heroes of antiquity have taken a stroll through Cat's Walk.[50]
DON LATINO: This is the drink talking!
MAX: The heroes of old reflected in distorting mirrors produce the *Esperpento.* The tragic sense of Spanish life can only be reproduced by an esthetic posited on systematic distortion.

. . . .

Spain is a grotesque deformation of European civilization . . . The most beautiful images are absurd when reflected in a concave mirror. . . . One can no longer speak of deformation when it becomes a mathematical calculation. My esthetic at the present time is to transform classical standards with the mathematical accuracy of a concave mirror.[51]

This passage can be taken as a direct and unequivocal declaration of intent. The most important points to be borne in mind are (a) The author considers Spain to be a grotesque distortion of European civilization; this prepares the reader for the withering satire of Spain typical of the *esperpento;* (b) The heroes of antiquity have taken a stroll through an alleyway flanked by distorting mirrors. Consequently, the protagonist of the *esperpento* plays will sometimes be a puny and grotesque parody of a classical hero; (c) Distortion is to be completely mathematical, that is, the *esperpento* will see the reversal of all orthodox human values. (Man is to be dehumanized by being visualized as a puppet, an animal or a bad actor, while concepts held dear by many, such as family love, patriotism and so forth, will be derided and ground beneath the author's heel); (d) The esthetic of the *esperpento* owes at least some of its inspiration to Goya. (Not to the Goya of the earlier Madrid scenes and the portraits of the aristocracy, but to the creator of the later *Caprichos* and *Disparates* with their depictions of dehumanized creatures, of madness, witchcraft, and inhuman savagery.)

It becomes evident from the summary given of the *esperpento's* purpose, that so far as the author is concerned there can be no quarter for his countrymen. Valle's satire is merciless; it is also destructive and negative in that no answers are provided for Spain's ills. There are, apparently, no remedies for the situation in which the country finds itself. The negative quality of the satire in the *esperpentos* is something for which Valle has often been reproached, but this does not appear to me a justifiable criticism. It is the task of the satirist to make others conscious of what he considers to be amiss; to create awareness and indignation in the face of social or other evils. He is the explorer who maps out the terrain; the colonizers should follow in his wake.

One more question should be considered before ending this chapter, namely the vexing one of the correct use of the term *esperpento*. The *esperpentos* themselves are in dramatic form, but the esthetic behind the *esperpento* is evident in all the works written by Valle-Inclán in the 1920's, either in the form of play or novel. Thus the term *esperpentización* can be applied with impunity to the narratives of the period. Valle-Inclán was himself quite explicit on this point. He once declared in an interview that he had turned from the dramatic form to the novel simply because the latter allowed him greater scope for the exposition of his ideas.[52] Consequently one should distinguish between a new genre and an attitude of mind. Of the two terms, *esperpento* and *esperpentización*, the second is the more far-reaching, for it colors all his later works. Any attempt at a rigid division is bound to be false.

CHAPTER 3

Some Fundamental Elements of
Valle-Inclán's Production

HAVING described in general terms the influences which helped to mold Valle-Inclán's esthetic, it is now my purpose to show what results these had on his works, dwelling initially on certain features which account for their originality. These I shall list in order, explaining each briefly.

I *Distortion and Violence*

It is an incontrovertible fact that distortion of both character and background is a fundamental aspect of all Valle-Inclán's works of fiction. For that matter the statement is equally applicable to his so-called "autobiographical" material which is often nothing other than bizarre fabrication.[1] As one critic has noted, there is simply no place in the author's production, regardless of phase, for the development of a fully rounded, "realistic" character.[2] He moves from an idealized vision of the world in the earlier *Sonatas* or *Flor de santidad (The Saintly Flower)* to a completely grotesque and debased one in the *esperpentos,* passing through an interim period in which the stylization of both characters and background is just as marked as in the other two. The reason for this stylization and the distortion which is its inevitable accompaniment is Valle-Inclán's belief that the material world is an illusion. Thus it is either ignored or else the writer feels free to distort it at will, for it is in any case ephemeral and without value.

Writing on current trends in the visual arts and literature, the Spanish philosopher Ortega y Gasset noted in 1925 that dehumanization is the single most significant feature of modern art forms.[3] He maintains also that dehumanization and stylization are indivisible. This statement is certainly applicable with no form of qualification to Valle's works of fiction. Admittedly, other points made by Ortega in the same essay are not relevant to the author under consideration. Chief among these is the notion that the tone of modern art is lighthearted, that art is being treated as a sophisticated game. Owing to the idea culled from the Gnostics that all matter is essentially evil, Valle-Inclán's outlook on the world is profoundly pessimistic.

Violence is as pronounced a characteristic of the author's major works as distortion.[4] What strikes the reader immediately is the marked contrast between the extreme subtlety of his thought and the indirect way in which it is expressed in his production with the constant presence of violence in both dialogue and action. Evidently, the quality of this violence changes according to the characters and their setting. In the *Sonatas* it is refined and ultrasophisticated, affected by a nonchalance and a detachment such as are evident in De Quincey's essay on "Murder as one of the Fine Arts." Later, in the trilogy *Comedias bárbaras (The Vandals)*, with their pseudo-medieval setting, violence takes the form of primitive brutality and cruelty. In the works of Valle's last period, violence is inevitably affected by the esthetic of the *esperpento*. This means that far from being condoned or lauded as it was in his *modernista* works, violence is seen as an intrinsic but degrading element of the society he depicts. Violence is now expressed through the parodic treatment of death and the periodic clashes between men that reflect the essentially evil nature of the sensible world. The most important point to be borne in mind is that violence is as integral to some of the author's very earliest short stories[5] as it is to his final work, the fragment of a future novel *El trueno dorado (Gilded Youth)*,[6] that he was unable to complete.

II *The World of Phenomena and the World of Ideas*

Since the outward world of appearances is deemed illusory, it follows that the author should aim to reflect archetypes or essences belonging to the superior world of Ideas. This is precisely what Valle-Inclán sets out to do in his works, and it accounts for his statement that he prefers characters who already possess an established literary background to characters of his own invention:

. . . the artist must contemplate the landscape from a lofty vantage point so as to encompass the whole of it and not the ever-changing details. If one tries to preserve in art that air of collective observation which one finds in folk literature, things acquire a beauty which stems from distance. For this reason one should depict characters by adding something which they have never had. Thus a beggar should resemble Job and a warrior Achilles.[7]

Apart from his very significant allusions to the need for archetypal figures, it is also interesting to note the emphasis Valle lays on distance: the artist must not be deluded by ephemeral detail; he must instead strive after a global picture, that is, he must aim to depict the essence and not its more superficial manifestations. Valle's endeavor to dispense at times with the world of phenomena accounts for the importance given to the blind in his work. They, as he indicates in *The Wonderful Lamp*, have a profounder understanding of the universe than those with sight, because they are not dazzled by the multiplicity of external matter and are less conscious of the error of chronological time.

One of the few critics to date who has shown an awareness of Valle-Inclán's use of archetypes and its implications is Eugenio Montes. In a lecture given in Madrid in 1944, he referred in passing to this extremely important aspect of Valle's art: "Valle-Inclán's characters do not belong to this century, to another or to any particular one. . . . They are to be found in an atemporal world of poetry and dream. Such characters are people in the dramatic and, perhaps, philosophic sense of the word, not individuals. For him people represent grades or planes of reality with different levels and forms of communion. A priest is in his eyes the Church . . . a peasant the countryside."[8]

Naturally enough this rejection of the external world has some interesting and unusual repercussions in Valle's works. For example, from a very early date he is apt to transfer a description of one character to a completely different one without altering a word of it. This is something noted by Professor Fichter in the study which precedes his collection of Valle-Inclán's early short stories and newspaper articles. Here Fichter observes that on two occasions Valle repeats a description in this way, despite the fact that in one case in particular, when he is talking of the Socialist politician Pablo Iglesias, the description transferred from another character does not fit him at all well.[9]

Valle-Inclán is also apt to transfer a character from one setting to a completely different one, giving him what is in effect a new identity but keeping the name he had used earlier. This is evident above all in terms of minor characters. Thus there are in his works a number of peasants called Serenín de Bretal[10] and a number of aristocrats called the Duke of Ordax[11] who keep reappearing in different guises and with a supreme disregard for chronology which is, of course, quite deliberate. Valle-Inclán is, in fact, utterly indifferent to chronology as both the *Sonatas* and *Bohemian Lights* bear out.[12] His attitude towards time relates to another aspect of his philosophy, namely that chronological time is false. Thus, just as Valle seeks to expose the illusion of individuality in his works, the same is true of his attitude to linear time.

III   *The Use of Set Phrases and the Reelaboration of Material*

Valle-Inclán is also in the habit of reelaborating earlier material and of repeating certain set phrases, akin to epic epithets. Apart from the fact that his custom of repeating stock expressions reflects the notion that the phenomena of the external world are illusory, it may also be owed to the fact that the phrases in question hold a particular significance for him; that is, the author is using them as symbols. This is particularly apparent in the case of certain set expressions used to describe effects of light. Again, the fact that these should relate to light is of interest in that, as has already been noted,[13] it had a particular significance for the author. Two cases which illustrate this point are, first, the reference to light glinting on a weapon and, second, the allusions to the cracked chimney of an oil lamp.

Light glinting on a weapon implies, as one would expect, a threat of violence or the imminence of death. In the historical novels written towards the end of Valle-Inclán's life, namely the *Ruedo ibérico (Iberian Ring)* cycle, precisely the same significance is given to a glint of light on the patent-leather headgear of the Civil Guards. To illustrate both these points, we offer three examples chosen at random from works belonging to both the earlier and later phases of Valle's writing career:

The bushes of the hedge stirred . . . and a black shadow leaped into the middle of the road . . . raising aloft a sickle which . . . shone for a moment with a sinister steely glint . . .[14]

Her troubled eyes closed tightly, dazzled by the light of the knife raised by the yellow specter of Don Igi. Pepona, half swooning, feels the young man's lips growing cold on hers.[15]

The Civil Guard, fierce with light on patent leather and weapons, came forward to bring peace with sundry blows from their rifle butts.[16]

The cracked chimney of an oil lamp, with its emblematic value, is just as much a set phrase—used as a form of incantation —as the gleam of light on a weapon or other object that brings death in its train. The chimney may suggest either the devil— due to the horn-shaped flame—or, by extension, a cuckold. There again, for greater clarity, it is best to illustrate the point by textual references. In the first case, a child realizes that his elder sister, Antonia, has been bewitched by a student who is in love with her:

Plunged in an abysmal ignorance of life, I guessed my sister Antonia's secret. I felt its oppressive weight on my soul like a mortal sin as I crossed the anteroom where smoke was rising from a lamp with a cracked chimney.[17]

The second example, from the finest *esperpento, Los Cuernos de don Friolera (Don Friolera's Horns),* involves cuckoldry. Lieutenant Rovirosa, an army officer, has come to tell his colleague Friolera about the decision of the military tribunal concerning his wife's presumed unfaithfulness:

A gust of sea wind enters the room . . . the flame of the oil lamp parts to form two horns. In the doorway with a hand to his glass eye is Lieutenant Rovirosa.[18]

The third example, taken from the verse collection *La Pipa de kif (The Marihuana Pipe),* involves not bewitchment or magic, but applies really to Valle-Inclán's Gnostic beliefs. However, it should be recalled that, according to the Gnostics, the temporal world is ruled by an evil power, the Demiurge, so that the dif-

ference is slight. What suggests Gnosticism in this quotation
is the use of the term *Ananké* (necessity to which the temporal
world is tied) and the reference to a circle whose significance
has already been noted:[19]

> The cat dozes in a chair
> The lamp casts a circular shadow on the ceiling
> The horned yellow light
> speaks in the room of *Ananké*.

It will have emerged from this brief consideration of Valle-
Inclán's use of archetypal figures and the repetition of certain
set phrases, that it is all too easy without prior understanding
of the author's philosophical leanings to form superficial judg-
ments about this aspect of his work. Indeed, many are the critics
who are guilty in this respect,[20] condemning his work as bookish,
effete and lacking in invention, unaware of the significance of
these repetitions and of his arbitrary treatment of individuality.

Since novelty in terms of character portrayal or background
is valueless because it relates only to the world of the senses,
the author must instead seek to perfect the stylized product he
has created or borrowed by submitting it to a scrupulous process
of elaboration. Valle-Inclán makes repeated use of the same
material, constantly delving into earlier works until they have
reached that stage of comparative perfection which satisfies the
author and thus becomes the final version. This tendency to
rewrite earlier material, like so many others, can be traced back
to his formative years as a writer. A few examples of this process
of reelaboration will serve to illustrate this point.

In his article "Sobre la génesis de la *Sonata de estío*,"[21] Fichter
has shown how certain descriptive passages from this more
mature work can be traced back through the short story "La
niña Chole" (*Feminine Cameos*) to the short descriptive article
"Bajo los trópicos. 1. En el mar," first published in Mexico in
1892.[22] Another critic who has rendered a similar service is
Emma Susana Speratti Piñero in her article "Génesis y evolución
de la *Sonata de otoño*."[23] In this article she sheds considerable
light on the development of the first *Sonata, Autumn,* by com-
menting on the various episodes later incorporated in the narrative, which had appeared initially in the magazine *Juventud*

and in the newspaper *El Imparcial*.[24] The short story "Adega," widened in scope, was to become the novel *Flor de santidad (Saintly Flower)*, and it is likely that another short story, "La reina de Dalicam" ("The Queen of Dalicam") of 1899 formed the basis of "Rosita" from *La corte de amor (The Court of Love)*, 1903.[25]

Valle used this very method of gradually developing relatively simple material with regard to a very different type of narrative, namely his account of the situation at the French front in 1916. The substance of his observations in the Alsace and Champagne regions is recorded firstly in letters addressed to a personal friend in Spain, and in notebooks where he jotted down his impressions.[26] The scope of these original notes and comments is then enlarged in a series of articles written for *El Imparcial* from October, 1916 to February, 1917. These, in turn, are subsequently developed into *A media noche (At Midnight)*, published in 1917. It appears from the brief foreword to this work that even the final draft left him dissatisfied: "These pages which now see the light of day are nothing but an incoherent mumble of the ideal I had envisaged. I shall return to France and to the battle front to purify my emotions, and who knows if I might not yet accomplish my lofty purpose of describing the visions and the emotions of A DAY OF WAR."[27] However, this project, like the ambitious scope of *The Iberian Ring* cycle, was not to be completed.

The genesis of the outstanding novel of the *esperpento* period, *Tirano Banderas (The Tyrant)*, follows the same familiar course. Here, as in the case of the *Autumn Sonata*, it is Speratti Piñero who has successfully traced the development.[28] This critic discovered that four chapters of the future novel were published independently in the June-July and December issues of the magazine *El estudiante* in 1925, and in the January-February number for 1926. These chapters were "El juego de la ranita" ("The game of *Ranita*"), "El honorable cuerpo diplomático" ("The Honourable Diplomatic Corps"), "Mitote revolucionario" ("Revolutionary Ferment") and "La mueca verde" ("The Green Grimace"). "Zacarías el Cruzado o Agüero nigromante" ("Zacharias the Scarred or The Necromantic Omen") was published in the collection *La novela de hoy* in September, 1926. The completed novel appeared in the same year. Here too, it becomes apparent from the early drafts which appeared in the periodical that modifications and improvements were made before these episodes came to be incorporated into the body of the novel. Certain incidents are switched from one locality to another. This was done to add an element of surprise, since in the original form the development of the plot had been somewhat mechanical. Comparisons of the earlier and final versions show, as was also to be the case with different drafts of the *Iberian Bull Ring* cycle, that the author was constantly searching for more colorful and exact expressions.

IV   The Structure of Valle-Inclán's Novels

I wish to consider the structure of a number of Valle-Inclán's novels under two headings. The first of these involves number symbolism and the author's Gnostic beliefs; the second relates to the essential modernity of the structure he imposes on his later narratives. In other words, I should like to relate the structure of Valle's later novels to that of certain contemporary writers in other countries, and to point out their affinities.

1.   Number symbolism

Recently certain critics have begun to notice that a variety of Valle-Inclán's novels have a rigorously symmetrical structure. In *Las estéticas de Valle-Inclán*, Guillermo Díaz-Plaja[29] points out that *The Wonderful Lamp* is built around a central book or section. The remaining sections are grouped about it in symmetrical order as follows:

> A Summary of the Comments
> The Musical Miracle
> Ternary Exegesis
> Esthetic Quietism
> The Philosopher's Stone

In a most illuminating article, Jean Franco[30] has shown how the completed novels of the *Iberian Ring*, that is, *The Court Of Miracles* and *Viva mi dueño (Hurrah for my Owner)* have a circular structure that is a manifestation of Valle's profound interest in Gnosticism. The circular structure imposed on these novels is especially obvious in *Hurrah for my Owner*, which begins and ends with precisely the same words by way of a jeering comment on the political chaos in Spain. Both these novels are divided into nine books in which a central book, number five, gives meaning to the whole and is flanked by four books on either side. Thematic parallels are established between 1 and 9, 2 and 8, 3 and 7, 4 and 6 by centering attention on the same characters and backcloths in each pair.

The Saintly Flower has a similar though less elaborate structure: once again there is a central book containing six chapters, flanked by four other books each consisting of five chapters. Thus 5 is the dominant number in this case, the reason being that *The Saintly Flower* shows Pantheistic leanings on the author's part and, according to Pythagorean number symbolism, the number 5 defines nature, embracing all living things. Thus there are five essences, five parts of musical harmonies, five inhabitants of the world (plants, fishes, animals, birds, humans) and five senses.[31] Finally, *Tirano Banderas (The Tyrant)* has a structure similar to the *Iberian Ring* cycle.[32]

It is *The Tyrant* which reveals the most intricate and fascinating structure. Not only is it circular, as is also the case with the *Iberian Ring* novels, thus relating it to Gnosticism; but it is also based on three and seven, numbers of vital importance in Pythagorean number symbolism; seven because it signifies the union of man and divinity, and three because man is composed of three elements, namely, body, soul, and spirit. The *Tyrant* is based on an inversion of time in which events related in the epilogue follow immediately on those narrated in the prologue, while the greater part of the book carries us back in time, filling in those details which account for the action of the revolutionaries in both prologue and epilogue. The structure of the main part of the narrative is as follows:

Part I, book 1: Ikon of the Tyrant
　　　　book 2: The Spanish Minister
　　　　book 3: The Game of *Ranita*
Part II, book 1: Iberian Quartz
　　　　book 2: The Harris Circus
　　　　book 3: The Fox's Ear
Part III, book 1: The Green Bedroom
　　　　book 2: Voices from the Dead

Of the four works mentioned, that is, *The Court of Miracles,
Hurrah for my Owner, The Saintly Flower* and *The Tyrant*, it
is without doubt the last-named and the two *Iberian Ring*
novels that are the most interesting examples of Valle's use of
number symbolism. This is firstly because they are the most
sophisticated examples of elaborate structures serving an ulterior
and arcane purpose, that is, the revealing of Valle's interest
in Gnosticism. The circular construction imposed on these
novels is the result of his belief that cyclic time dominates the
sensible world and that events repeat themselves at periodic
intervals.[33] All three of these novels defy man-made notions of
time: instead of unfolding the plot in chronological fashion,
Valle-Inclán describes a number of events which are to be
interpreted as occurring simultaneously. Both *The Tyrant* and
The Court of Miracles are long novels, yet the action in the
former is limited to a period of forty-eight hours (the religious
festivals of All Saints and All Souls), while the action in the
latter covers a period of nine days; from the ceremony of the
Golden Rose in Book One on Easter Sunday (April 12, 1868)
to the death of the Prime Minister, Narváez, in the last Book
(April 21, 1868).

As is so often the case with Valle-Inclán, such ideas took a long time to mature in his works. It is obvious from the stylized framework of *The Saintly Flower* that both number symbolism and its application to the structure of a narrative had intrigued him from an early date. Further evidence pointing in the same direction is found in a letter Valle wrote in 1909 addressed to an imaginary critic whom he styles "Don Fantasio." Apparently Valle felt rather peeved at this time because his novel *Gerifaltes de antaño (Gerfalcons of Yore)*, 1908-1909, had come under fire from certain critics who considered it amorphous and fragmentary. In this letter[34] Valle sets out to prove that the very reverse is the case: *Gerfalcons of Yore* has an elaborate structure resembling that used years later in the *Iberian Ring* novels and *The Tyrant*. Like them, *Gerfalcons of Yore* has a central chapter with others flanking it and deliberate parallels established between them. Thus the guerrilla leader Manuel Santa Cruz who is in the forefront in chapters one and two, also has an essential part in chapters thirty-three and thirty-four. Chapters three and four, devoted to the Government forces, are paralleled by thirty-one and thirty-two, in which the Government forces are once again in the foreground. Valle ends by saying that for rather trivial reasons he decided to merge chapters thirty-three and thirty-four, thus marring the symmetry of the whole.

Although Valle-Inclán stresses the fact that the framework of this novel is based on a pyramid—with chapter seventeen at the apex and chapters one and thirty-four as the base—it is easy to see how once he became interested in Gnosticism, the same structure could be conceived as circular with the central chapter forming the center of the circle. With regard to the two completed novels of the *Iberian Ring* there can be little doubt as to this, since the general title indicates a circle. In addition, there are frequent allusions to the circle which symbolizes temporal condition and chronological time in the novels themselves, this being the case also with *The Wonderful Lamp*.

It might be maintained, as many critics tend to when speaking of the more esoteric aspects of the Symbolists and their spiritual descendants, that this application of number symbolism is puerile and hermetic. If it is the main purpose of a writer to communicate, why then should he play such elaborate games with the reader? Why couldn't Valle simply have stated that he was interested in Gnosticism and number symbolism? To this

there is only one answer: Valle-Inclán believed implicitly that
the author should never intrude in the narrative, but should
make his point indirectly. The idea of the omnipotent author
of whose presence in a novel one is constantly aware was ab-
horrent to him. This is why he came to rely increasingly on
dialogue in his later works, cutting down descriptions to a bare
but effective minimum.

2. *The Twentieth-Century Approach to the Structure of the
   Novel.*

Valle-Inclán's evident interest in the structure of the novel is
a reflection of a very general preoccupation among authors of
the period under consideration, which continues to the present
day. Like his contemporaries, Valle was seeking to render the
novel infinitely more flexible than its nineteenth-century predecessor. The rejection of chronological time is a further aspect
of his later novels which reflects a very general preoccupation
with the subject from the early years of the century.[35] Its philosophic basis lay in an altered attitude to time, which was viewed
cyclically and not chronologically as had been the case from the
Renaissance onwards. Its most obvious manifestations are to be
found in the works of the Simultanists—Apollinaire, Joyce, Virginia Woolf—who sought to grasp the moment in its total significance, or to manufacture a moment that contained eternity
through sheer intensification of the present. Thus if Valle-Inclán's
later novels are considered in a wider context, it will be seen
that he is not adopting an eccentric attitude towards the structure
of the novel; rather, he was but one of a number of writers who
were rebelling against the narrow confines of the well-made
novel, to which pattern a majority of novelists had adhered in
the previous century.

Qualms about the future of the novel are expressed by José
Ortega y Gasset in his essay *Ideas sobre la novela (Ideas on the
Novel).*[36] In it he asks himself if the novel is falling inevitably
into a state of decline. He maintains that formerly the novelty
of a plot was sufficient to engage and keep the reader's attention,
but that now all stories of interest and originality have been
exhausted. Thus, due to the growing sophistication of the reading
public, an author is forced increasingly to dwell on the characters
and the subtleties of their reactions to events in the plot. The

novelist must also endeavor to see that his characters develop with a minimum of intrusion from the author himself: "It . . . is necessary that we should see the life of fictional characters and that their description by the author should be avoided. Everything indicated, related, or narrated only stresses the absence of what is indicated, related, or narrated."[37] A very similar point of view is expressed by James Joyce in *Portrait of the Artist as a Young Man,* when Stephen Dedalus is speaking to his friend Lynch about the lyric, epic, and dramatic forms in art. Of the last-named Stephen makes the following remarks: "The esthetic image in the dramatic form is life purified in and re-projected from the human imagination. The mystery of esthetic like that of material creation is accomplished. The artist, like the God of the creation, remains within or beyond or behind his handiwork, invisible, refined out of existence, indifferent, paring his fingernails."[38]

Thus Valle and Joyce agree on the need for dramatic form in the novel: the novelist may be omniscient in the fictional world of his own creation, but he must not be omnipresent. Where the writers differ is in the methods they employ to turn theory into practice. Joyce, like Virginia Woolf, favors the interior monologue, while Valle exteriorizes his characters by employing a maximum of dialogue with short, impressionistic descriptions to introduce and round off individual scenes. It is only infrequently that Valle resorts to a stream-of-consciousness technique to achieve particular effects.[39]

The desire Valle expressed in an interview to avoid the use of a central character in the *Iberian Ring* novels is something else that links him with a number of contemporary writers.[40] Dos Passos' *Manhattan Transfer* (1925), Joyce's *Ulysses* (1922), and Virginia Woolf's *Mrs. Dalloway* (1925) are the products of other novelists of the period who, like Valle, sought to break away from the limitations of the well-constructed novel. No longer does the author restrict himself to describing the fortunes of a few individuals through a series of situations presented in chronological fashion; instead he chooses to explore the wider reaches of society, availing himself of a large number of characters to achieve his purpose.

It could be argued that this concentration on society as opposed to the individual was hardly an innovation, for authors such as Zola, Tolstoy, Balzac and Galdós had done precisely this in the previous century.

However, they differ from their twentieth-century counterparts in the technical and stylistic aspects of their craft. In the first place, characters introduced by these earlier authors in a given novel were almost invariably brought to bear on a specific dramatic issue. This is by no means the case in the novels of the more recent generation, where characters may simply be introduced to add density or credibility to a given situation. Another feature which separates the two groups of novelists is the obsession of the more recent one with the problem of time. The plot in a novel by Pérez Galdós will be unfolded chronologically, perhaps covering a period of years; the tendency shown by the more recent group is to present a multitude of thoughts, actions and sensations, disordered and chaotic as in life itself, which should often be apprehended as occurring simultaneously. This is the case with *Ulysses,* whose entire action takes place in less than twenty-four hours, and with *The Tyrant* where the events described, as I mentioned earlier, are limited to a period of two days.

This endeavor to capture everything in a chaotic present on which order can only be imposed when juxtaposed parts are seen to be occurring simultaneously, is one of the most revolutionary features of modern art. Up to the early years of this century, painting and literature had been governed by the classical concept of unity: these were arts of transition and not of juxtaposition. Thus, in painting, the artist was ever conscious of perspective, and in drama, the playwright ensured that each part should follow inevitably from the last. The twentieth-century artist turned instead to disconcerting and fragmentary arts of juxtaposition in which anticipation, as in a tragedy by Racine, is replaced by surprise as in a "Calligramme" by Apollinaire or a Cubist painting by Braque or Picasso.[41]

It is unnecessary to elaborate further on the effects which these newly-developed arts of juxtaposition exercised on the structure of Valle's novels and on those of many contemporary writers. The emphasis shifted from a strict sequence of events giving meaning to the whole, to a series of "images," described by Ezra Pound as "that which presents an intellectual and emotional complex in an instant of time." This stress on a diversity of events, together with the technique of the film which uses juxtaposed details in a montage construction, account to a considerable extent for the structure of Valle's later novels. He has often been criticized for the supposed formlessness of his novels, but critics mistake a lack of orthodox form for a lack of any form whatsoever. The structure of the *Iberian Ring* novels and *The Tyrant* is, rather, very formal indeed, as is also the case with another apparently disjointed and haphazard work, Joyce's *Ulysses*.

CHAPTER 4

The Poetry of Valle-Inclán

R ATHER than considering the author's works in chronological order, I intend to divide them into three genres,
poetry, drama and the novel, dwelling on each one in turn and
tracing its development. Poetry will be the first to be studied
since it will require the least space for its elucidation. This is
largely because poetry does not occupy a significant position
in Valle's production, although one qualification must be made:
each one of the three collections to be considered, *Aromas de
leyenda (The Aromas of Legend)*, *La pipa de kif (The Marihuana
Pipe)* and *El pasajero (The Passenger)*, has an evident bearing
on other works with which it is contemporaneous. Thus *The
Aromas of Legend* (1907) reflects the same spirit as, say, *The
Saintly Flower*. *The Marihuana Pipe* (1919) announces the esthetic of the *esperpento*, while the poems of *The Passenger* (1920)
relate to the interest in esoteric doctrines evident in *The
Wonderful Lamp*. It is obvious from the contents of these
poems that many of them were written a few years before the
collection was published. Possibly, according to his common
practice, Valle-Inclán published some of them independently
in literary journals before the appearance of *The Passenger*.

When asked by a fellow poet, Gerardo Diego, to express his
views on poetry,[1] Valle stated that he thought there was no
obvious demarcation line between poetry and prose. Certainly,
this is the impression derived from his own production for,
if anything, the prose is much more "poetic" than the actual
poetry. Perhaps at this juncture it would be advisable to define
my terms. By poetic in this particular context I do not mean
language that is deliberately consciously artificial language
aloof from prose but, rather, a line, phrase or sentence which
partly through its appeal to the ear and partly owing to its

original and well-nigh inimitable wording suggests and conveys far more than the words themselves would warrant. In short, the reader feels this is perhaps the finest way in which a particular thought or sensation can be rendered. It is a word or phrase whose content is so compressed that one can return to it time after time and still detect another shade of meaning which had previously passed unnoticed. Such a sensation is common enough in Valle-Inclán's prose, but rarer in his poetry. It is my own opinion that the formal meters he favored inhibited his talents in this direction. Had he attempted free verse instead, the result would probably have been far more successful, but he does not appear to have made any such attempt, and certainly none was ever published.

I Aromas de leyenda (1907)

The poems in this collection consist of a nostalgic, idealized evocation of Galicia written by Valle in distant Madrid. The poems are written in orthodox Spanish meters and, in a number of them, Valle uses the traditional *romance* or ballad meter consisting of lines of eight syllables with assonance in every second line which is kept throughout the poem. Both the use of a traditional verse form and the introduction of refrains in Galician to round off the majority of these poems, betray a very obvious interest in popular poetry common to many twentieth-century Spanish poets.

Valle concentrates in these poems on either the hidalgos (country gentry) of Galicia or the truly wretched. There are at least three poems, "Los pobres de Dios" ("God's Poor"), "Dolor" ("Sorrow") and "Lirio franciscano" ("Franciscan Lily") concerned with the beggar bands that travelled the roads of Galicia. These also figure prominently in his earlier prose works. However, even the descriptions of their sores and deformities are idealized so that the total effect is not of ugliness but of beauty.[2]

The appeal to the senses, particularly through visual and auditory effects, is the single most obvious feature of these poems, but there are three poems which have a certain bearing on Valle's attitude to time. They concern a reworking of the medieval legends about the doubting monk of the monastery at Heisterbach, and the friar in the *Cantigas de Santa Maria*[3]

who asked the Virgin if he might have an anticipation of
Heaven. The Virgin grants him the request and the humble
friar spends three hundred years listening to a bird's song. In this
case the monk or friar becomes a hermit, San Gundián who,
in the poem "Prosa de dos ermitaños" ("Conversation Between
Two Hermits") expresses a fervent desire to pierce the veil of
mystery surrounding life. In the final poem, "Estela de prodigio"
("The Return"), the hermit returns to the finite world to discover
that three hundred years have elapsed and that two angels are
digging his grave.

There is one further significant point in these poems. In the
penultimate one, "Sol de la tarde" ("Afternoon Sun"), there
are two lines reflecting the Traditionalist views so dear to Valle
at this time. Speaking of old men in a village taking the afternoon
sun, he writes that they resemble ". . . judges of bygone days
when judges did not exist and tradition was the fount of all
wisdom."[4]

Nature appears lush and verdant, its soft contours recalling
those of a woman in a description with a markedly erotic
flavor: "The rustic way undulates between two small, fragrant
hills, like two upright breasts, with the roundness of apples."[5]
The atmosphere evoked in these poems is precisely the same
as that in the novel *The Saintly Flower*, which is their obvious
complement. There is the same interest in the two extremes of
Galician society—squire and beggar—the same idealization of the
landscape; and identical interest in the language of the peasants
and in their superstitions. It must be admitted, however, that
the novel is much more rewarding than the poems which seldom
rise above the level of mediocrity.

II La pipa de kif

A radical change of direction in his approach to literature
is announced by Valle-Inclán with great brio in the second
poem of this collection called appropriately enough, "Hallelujah!"
Freely translated, the most significant lines from this poem read
as follows: "Spring has made me a creature of whims,/ I feel
the urge to write crazy, clownish verse/ a purist would call them
outrageous/ for 'respectable' people they are the most shocking
sport. . . . might not this grotesque muse/ —I'll now dispense
with the clownish— which exasperates the fuddy-duddy rhetori-

cians/ with its spasmodic shouts/ and jumps about baring its legs,/ be the modern muse?"[6] A very similar thought finds its more perfect expression in some lines of verse serving to introduce a play which is the direct predecessor of the *esperpento.* This is the *Farsa de la reina castiza (Farce of the Castilian Queen),* where the author writes "My modern muse/ kicks her legs,/ flashy and provocative she sways, curves and whirls/ with the rhythmic flourishes/ of the tango/ and lifts up her skirt at the back."[7]

Evident here is a mood of playfulness, youthful zest, self-confidence and something akin to cheek. It is worth noting in passing that one of the features Ortega y Gasset considers of great importance in modern art forms is its playfulness: art is being treated as a sophisticated game.[8] This is precisely the impression derived from "Hallelujah" and from the *Farce of the Castilian Queen.* Admittedly, Valle's outlook was to be soured by certain political events in the early twenties, and the mood reflected in the major works of the *esperpento* period is altogether different.

There are a number of very interesting features in *The Marihuana Pipe* most of which, inevitably, refer to the formulation of Valle's new esthetic. One important point is that his attention is now focused on the city, Madrid, and not on rural Galicia as had been the case in *Aromas of Legend.* Furthermore, his outlook is no longer aristocratic: he concentrates on the dregs of urban society and on the slum quarters of the city. When a member of the Galician squirearchy is introduced, as in the poem "The Lady of Medinica Manor," the character in question receives short shrift from the poet, being visualized as a grasping and narrow-minded provincial. Certain of the poems in *The Marihuana Pipe* reveal that there has been a marked change in the painters who appeal to Valle-Inclán. Whereas the *Sonatas* are peppered with allusions to the Italian Primitives and to the Renaissance masters, he now reveals an interest in Goya's "dark" paintings and the grim and austere vision of the modern Spanish painter Gutiérrez Solana.[9]

There is one series of poems, those set in the town of Medinica, which is very interesting as an exercise in structure. These poems show the author experimenting with a type of framework he was to employ in the finest *esperpento, Don Friolera's Horns.* Here

a story is related from two different angles. Firstly, a scene is
set; we learn about doña Estefaldina, a spinster who is the most
important citizen of Medinica, then of the ne'er-do-well who
is her maid's lover. In time this individual kills doña Estefaldina
and is led to prison amid the jeers of the populace. Finally he
is garrotted in the town square. Up to this point we have been
given a detached and objective account of the events. However,
these narrative poems are followed by one called "El Crimen de
Medinica" ("The Crime of Medinica"), which provides the
"popular" version. This is a blind man's song in which the events
recounted would be illustrated by the singer with the aid of a
colored board divided into squares resembling a giant strip
cartoon. Thus the story is told in dramatic form and is divided
into scenes. Not only is it dramatic; it is also lurid and highly
colored so as to appeal to the popular imagination. "Mother!
such cries from the bandit! / Dead! What a desperate embrace! /
Blood! A stream of it at her feet!"[10] Evident in this series of
poems is the *mirada de soslayo,* or sidelong glance, which reflects
more than one angle of a particular event. Irony has been
defined as the ability to see more than one point of view at the
same time. Thus it is evident that this "sidelong glance" and
irony go hand in hand. In fact, it could be said that the *mirada
de soslayo* is the artistic manifestations of irony. Certainly, both
are much to the fore in Valle's *esperpentos.*

One poem which reveals Valle-Inclán's untiring interest in
violence is the stark and dramatic "Marina norteña" (Northern
Seascape") which both stylistically and in terms of the atmosphere evoked is in harmony with the *esperpentos* intended for
the theater. One stanza of the poem shows his interest in avant-
garde movements in the arts and in their revolutionary esthetics:
"The sad symphony of things / shouts Futurist-like in the afternoon / the conquest is announced of fresh emotions and new
esthetic creeds."[11]

One final point I should like to establish is that certain of
these poems reveal Valle's interest in techniques of dehumanization which were to become a pronounced feature of the major
works of the *esperpento* period. Valle-Inclán had tended from
his very earliest writings to visualize characters as animals, puppets or actors. The analogies involving actors are usually limited
to town dwellers since Valle seemed to consider hypocrisy an
essentially urban vice. The animal images could be flattering;

for example, he was apt to write of women in terms of birds or members of the cat family so as to suggest playfulness or lithe movements. Similarly, animal analogies applied to men could suggest nobility, courage or the primitive thrust and vitality Valle considered virtues in the earlier phase of his writing career. Puppet metaphors too were not necessarily used to coarsen or debase his creations, but merely to evoke the stylized pose of a doll. In the *esperpento* period Valle came to rely increasingly on these techniques of dehumanization as one very effective way of expressing his views indirectly on the society portrayed. As they come into prominence, so also they acquire greater originality and range. Not only are human beings dehumanized but, so as to make the distortion "mathematical," human attributes are given to animals and objects. In this way Valle-Inclán underscores the topsy-turvy nature of the world he is depicting.

These techniques of dehumanization, particularly those involving the use of animals to assist the process, are much to the fore in the poems of *The Marihuana Pipe*. An interesting use of the device is to be found in the poem "El circo de lona" ("The Big Top") in which he speaks of one of the women in the circus troupe as having a pigeon's breast and the haunch of a royal mare.[12] As from the appearance of the *Farce of the Castilian Queen* in 1919, these images are applied almost exclusively to Queen Isabel II who, as her portraits reveal, was a rather portly sovereign.

In almost every way imaginable the poems of *The Marihuana Pipe* are in direct contrast to those of *Aromas of Legend*. However, in both volumes the appeal is largely restricted to the senses, and one is conscious of distinct and conflicting artistic atmospheres. In the last book of poems to be considered, Valle is much more concerned with the formulation of his personal philosophy than with either style or the reflection of an artistic ambience.

III   El pasajero (1920)

By no means do all the poems in this collection reflect Valle-Inclán's interest in esoteric sciences or white magic. Some of them, like the very fine "Rosa de Túrbulos" ("Rose of Túrbulos") —an exotic and original description of a Maya princess—are purely decorative; in others Valle embroiders on his life as is his wont:[13] some betray the same hankering for the green pastures and diffused light of Galicia as do the poems of *Aromas of Legend,* while in yet another he describes the peasants of Castile in terms very reminiscent of Unamuno.[14] Nearly all these poems include the word "rose" in their titles. The rose does not have its usual emblematic significance for Valle-Inclán: it symbolizes neither beauty nor mutability. Instead, here, as in *The Wonderful Lamp,* it represents sex, fertility and, by extension, the world of the senses. For, according to Schopenhauer, on whom, as we have seen, Valle's idea is based, it is through the sexual urge that the Will finds its most obvious expression.

One poem of key significance is "Rosa Gnóstica" (Gnostic Rose") which reveals the Gnostic attitude toward time. Here Valle declares that the concept of chronological time is fallacious and that a single moment may contain eternity:

> Nothing will be which has not already been
> Nothing will be which will not be again
> All the instants filtering through the sand-glass
> are the equivalent of Eternity.[15]

He also refers to Time being the work of Satan and speaks of God as the Present. In this poem he touches on Plato's Cave allegory.[16] This allegory, which held an evident fascination for the Symbolists, is referred to once more in the poem "Asterisk."[17]

The tenth "rose," "La rosa del sol ("The Rose of the Sun"), relates to the Pythagorean's visualization of the sun as the link between man and the superior world. In the third stanza of this poem Valle writes: "The sun is the burning fountain which spills the Eternal Ideas into a human mold through the fiery lip of its mouth."[18]

It will have become evident, even from this cursory examination of the poems of *The Passenger,* that they bear an intimate relation to the contents of *The Wonderful Lamp.* There is precisely the same interest in the philosophic school of Alexandria, in Plato's doctrine of Forms and in cabalistic ritual. Thus, in their separate ways, each one of the three collections considered is closely linked to the rest of his work. However, as I have already mentioned, Valle-Inclán's poetry—with certain exceptions—is not of outstanding quality and is mostly of interest to the student of Valle-Inclán for the light it sheds on significant aspects of his work.

CHAPTER 5

The Earlier Dramas of Valle-Inclán

REGARDLESS of their genre, the majority of Valle-Inclán's works reveal a dramatic bias. This is due, as I have already mentioned, to the author's firm belief that characters should be allowed to develop with a minimum of intrusion on the author's part. Naturally, this dramatic tendency takes different forms in his production, as Valle's style evolves from *Modernismo* to *esperpento.* In the *Sonatas,* as a Spanish critic has noted, the characters appear to behave as though they were on stage in the presence of an audience. Their movements and poses are studied and they are often visualized as though making an obvious entrance or exit during the course of a "scene."[1]

If anything, this tendency to look on his creations as actors in a play becomes more marked in Valle-Inclán's later novels where the characters are often described as bad actors in a cheap melodrama. What applies to the foreground is true also of the background. These works contain consciously artificial effects of light, and bald lists of the objects in a room or items of dress after the manner of stage directions.

From a very early date Valle-Inclán showed a profound interest in the theater, to the extent that he himself was not averse to acting in either a professional or amateur capacity.[2] A further indication of his theatrical bent is the fact that he married an actress and accompanied her on a tour of certain Spanish-American states with a theatrical company. He was also well acquainted with the then famous Spanish actress María Guerrero although, unfortunately, their relationship was finally marred by a dispute over the production of one of Valle's plays.[3]

Valle-Inclán's first play, whose title was *Cenizas (Ashes),* was first published in 1899 and staged in Madrid in the same year. It was not well received. The failure of the play is ex-

plained by the simple fact that it is poor in quality. Thus it
is rather surprising to discover that, undeterred, Valle reissued
the play in 1907 under the fresh title of *El yermo de las almas
(The Waste Lands of the Soul)*. There is a certain irony in the
fact that later in life Valle was to pour merciless scorn on plays
written precisely after the fashion of his own *Ashes*. It is worth
giving a very brief summary of the plot so as to understand the
point of the satire in the later *esperpentos*.

Ashes is a tribute to the then popular playwright José de
Echegaray who was the apologist of Victorian-type middle-class
mores. His dramas concern conventional morality, the dire results
of adultery; inner conflicts resulting from guilt or divided loyal-
ties; revenge, and so forth. Furthermore, they are colored by a
goodly dose of sentimentality which is typical of the period.
Valle-Inclán's *Ashes*, then, follows the pattern established by
Echegaray, a pattern which had also served him in some of his
first short stories.[4] The play concerns a married woman in love
with an artist. She is afflicted by that fashionable nineteenth-
century disease, tuberculosis. The heroine feels the twin pull of
her family on the one hand (there are, inevitably, a sweet lisping
child and a stern, upright mother) and the deep attraction exercised on her by her bohemian lover. Finally, weakened not only
by disease but by such strong emotional pressures, she expires.

Such a curt summary probably makes the play for latter-day
audiences appear more naïve than it is in fact; yet there is
no denying that it is a highly derivative essay in conventional
morality: what one critic has termed Valle's "morbid, sentimental drama."[5] Such a play is rare in Valle's production and
it is hardly surprising that, given his satiric bent, he should
later have reacted so sharply against the *comedias burguesas*
of Echegaray which, on this occasion, he had chosen to imitate.

I The Comedias bárbaras

After the failure of *Ashes*, Valle seems to have lost interest
in the theater. But once married to Josefina Blanco, and perhaps
owing to her influence, he wrote three armchair plays under the
general title of *Comedias bárbaras (The Vandals)*. These plays
are really dramatic novels and, although by no means impossible to stage,[6] raise some tricky problems for the producer
because of their frequent scene shifts, the number of actors

involved, and the variety of actions which take place on stage. Two of the plays belonging to the trilogy were written between 1907 and 1909, while the third, which chronologically precedes the other two, was written in 1922. The two earlier plays are *Aguila de blasón (The Eagle Scutcheon)* and *Romance de lobos (The Ballad of the Wolves)*. The last part of the trilogy, *Cara de plata (Silver Face)*, is of special interest in that it shows how the *esperpento* has affected his style even if not, on this occasion, his subject matter.

A number of features in these plays are worth noting. The first is the importance of their social content. It emerges from the works of two other Galicians, the novelist Emilia Pardo Bazán and the poet Curro Enriques, that Galicians felt a sense of disquiet in the latter half of the nineteenth century because of the breakdown of the traditional social structure of rural Galicia. This structure was based on the supremacy of the local squire, who was expected to act in a patriarchal capacity towards his humbler and poorer fellows. Charity was shown to the bands of beggars who roamed the countryside, and protection was given to the squire's tenants when they were menaced from the outside.

It is obvious that this strictly hierarchical and paternalistic system is but a modified version of feudalism. However, from about the third decade of the nineteenth century a new stratum of the community began to make its presence felt in Spain. There came into prominence a middle class of lawyers, notaries, administrators, and so forth, who tended to resemble, at least in Valle's eyes, the "carpetbaggers" who took advantage of the landowning classes in the South after the Civil War. This rapacious middle class started to encroach on the power of the weakened Galician squirearchy. Thus Valle-Inclán's trilogy can be described as a heartfelt lament for the decline of the rural nobility of Galicia, a class to which the author felt he belonged by right.

The protagonist of this trilogy is the virile, atavistic don Juan Manuel Montenegro. Whatever his faults may be—and they are many—he is fundamentally upright and abides by his own well delineated moral code. For example, he is a true Christian in his attitude to the humble and the weak and practices charity towards the truly wretched. What one is given to understand

about this character is that the times are out of joint for him.
Don Juan Manuel's qualities, his vigor, boldness and generosity
of heart have no outlet in the nineteenth century. He and his
ilk are like prehistoric saurians doomed to extinction because
they are unable to adapt to a changed set of circumstances. The
decline of the stock is evident in five of his six sons. Barring
Miguel, who thanks to his comely appearance is known as
Cara de Plata (Silver Face), all don Juan Manuel's sons are
degenerate, corrupt and vicious. Farruquiño who is to take
Holy Orders is, perhaps, the most evil of the brothers and
utterly cynical about the priesthood.

Valle-Inclán conceived of don Juan Manuel as the Galician
Don Juan.[7] This is a point he makes clear in an interesting
letter sent to the literary journal *España* in 1924. In this letter
Valle explains that his purpose in the *The Vandals* was to renew
the Galician element of the Don Juan legend. He feels that the
chief characteristics of the Galician Don Juan are sacrilege and
irreverence towards the dead. But, the author continues, by
dint of disbelief, by provoking and feigning death, it comes,
and *The Ballad of the Wolves,* which crowns the trilogy, com-
mences. Death arrives heralded by omens and shipwrecks, with
punishments and remorse in train. These, which Valle considers
the most important characteristics of the original Galician Don
Juan, are what he is seeking to depict in *The Vandals.*

One more point must be emphasized before considering
these plays in more detail, namely their atavism. Although the
events narrated take place in the second half of the nineteenth
century, the atmosphere evoked is definitely that of the Middle
Ages; something that is brought out not only by the primitive
nature of the characters, but also by the numerous allusions in
stage directions to bygone times. This is no doubt meant to reinforce the contrast between the social class considered as it used
to be at the height of its vitality and its sad decline in modern
times.

a. Cara de plata (1922)

Although written many years after the two other parts,
Silver Face is, chronologically, the first. It is difficult to determine
why Valle-Inclán should have returned to the theme of the
Montenegro clan and their decline after so long an interval.

Perhaps, as a result of the importance he attached to the number three,[8] he felt a measure of dissatisfaction at having produced only two plays involving the same characters. Again, although he was inclined in the *esperpento* period to avoid his own region, it yet exercised a strong enough fascination on him to account for the occasional weakening of his determination to concentrate on the wider reaches of Spain.

As the title itself suggests, Silver Face, who figures not at all in *The Ballad of the Wolves* and only intermittently in *The Eagle Scutcheon,* is, together with his father, the most prominent character in the play. At the outset the position is as follows: don Juan Manuel believes that some of the peasants in the area have testified against him in court. Angered by this action, he is determined to deny them the right of way through his estate which acts as a shortcut to the neighboring village of Viana del Prior. In their turn the peasants are indignant at the squire's intransigent action, but are not resolute enough to fight him on their own. However, they find a staunch ally and a natural leader in the Abbot of Lantañón who determines to see that their rights are upheld. To this end the abbot decides that his niece Sabel (who has been staying with the Montenegros because she is don Juan Manuel's goddaughter) must return to his house forthwith. Sabel is an attractive young woman who is being roughly wooed by both don Juan Manuel—a notorious womanizer in the area—and his son Silver Face. The son makes obvious advances which Sabel counters with an unequivocal "Love me within the bounds of decency."[9] At one point she finds herself alone in a church at twilight when the village idiot, Fuso Negro, attempts to rape her. She is rescued by don Juan Manuel, who carries her back to his manor house. At this juncture the abbot arrives to claim his niece. Sabel refuses to leave, for now the strong attraction felt for her godfather has surfaced. It is inevitable that she should become the next in his long succession of mistresses. Enraged, the abbot decides that to avenge himself on the nobleman he will even consider a sacrilegious action. To this end he asks his sacristan to feign that he is dying so that he may contravene don Juan Manuel's ban by crossing his estate to take the Last Sacrament to the dying man. The pusillanimous sacristan agrees to his plan albeit with misgivings. This results in a superbly orchestrated parody of death complete with the traditional laments of his wife and tribe of children who chant in Galician "Oh, dear father, Oh sweet father, Oh poor father."[10] When the sacristan sees the lights of the funeral procession approaching his house he feels that matters are getting out of hand: he panics and confesses that his health is quite normal.

In the meanwhile Silver Face has learned that his father has seduced Sabel. Blind with jealousy he determines to kill him. The various threads are drawn together in the last and highly dramatic scene. The abbot approaches with the mourners and is stopped by don Juan Manuel. Silver Face rides in with an axe raised aloft, planning to kill his father. But don Juan Manuel is able to dissuade him by reasoned argument. Then the struggle between the abbot and don Juan Manuel reaches its culmination. Once don Juan Manuel has confessed to all the grievous sins he has committed in the past, he snatches the chalice from the abbot's hands. All those present recoil in horror as don Juan Manuel announces solemnly "I think I am the devil."[11]

It will be noted from this brief summary that the *Comedias bárbaras* are indeed aptly named, and that in *Silver Face* Valle is delineating what he considers to be the essential features of the Galician Don Juan. There is the feigning of death, the irreverence, and the element of sacrilege. Also evident is Valle-Inclán's love of violent juxtapositions: the attempted rape of Sabel takes place in a church under the eyes of the saints; don Juan Manuel, who considers himself the devil, wrests the ciborium from the abbot and, finally, the abbot, himself a man of God, is prepared to commit sacrilege to obtain his own ends. As I have already stated, violence is one of the unifying elements in Valle-Inclán's production. Nor, as will shortly become apparent, is *Silver Face* exceptional in this respect within the scope of *The Vandals*.

b. Aguila de blasón

It is rather difficult to provide a clear and succinct summary of the events in this play because it is, in effect, plotless. That is, there are numerous incidents but they do not necessarily follow any particular order or lead to a preconceived end. Valle believed that the times were ripe for a new approach to the stage: the plot of a play should be considered of little consequence and the emphasis laid on plastic elements and on an appeal to the senses. What he was searching for was a lyrical drama.

The first scene in the play takes place in a church where a friar is delivering a fire-and-brimstone sermon whose theme is adultery. Overcome by guilt, Sabel falls unconscious. After she returns home don Jaun Manuel arrives, but states categorically that the doors are to be kept barred because he is surrounded by bandits who intend to ransack his house. However, neither Sabel nor don Juan Manuel's dedicated servant Micaela la Roja is able to summon enough courage to do as he bids. Thus the bandits enter together with the squire. The ruffians then try to force Sabel to tell them where don Juan Manuel's gold is hidden. The nobleman enters armed with two pistols which he fires. The bandits return the fire, but alarmed by the pandemonium they exit while the going is still good.

Don Juan Manuel is sunk in gloom because he feels that the bandits were none other than his five sons. He says mournfully to his aged retainer Micaela la Roja that he is the last nobleman of his stock and she the last loyal servant. Don Juan Manuel's estranged wife, the virtuous doña María, arrives to plead for her sons; she cannot believe they are guilty of so heinous a crime. On seeing her, Sabel implores doña María's forgiveness and resolves to quit don Juan Manuel's house. He, undeterred, consoles himself with the miller's wife, Liberata la Blanca.[12] The local constable and the notary arrive to ask don Juan Manuel to testify about the robbers. He refuses to comply with this request and says he recognizes no law on his estate save his own. To reinforce his point he symbolically flings an inkpot out of the window and the representatives of law and order promptly take an undignified departure.

In the meanwhile the sons have not been idle. Silver Face (who is being pestered by a moneylender) and his brother Farruquiño decide to desecrate a graveyard by digging up a corpse. Their idea is to boil it down and sell the skeleton for ready cash. The plan is carried into effect. As the corpse bubbles in a pot, Silver Face makes love to a prostitute, La Pichona. At the same time another son, Pedrito, has set his dogs on Liberata la Blanca whom he then rapes. Silver Face decides that he must leave home and in a moving scene he bids farewell to his mother. He is determined to join the Carlist forces, for the second Carlist War is in progress.

When Sabel makes her escape at nightfall, she is accosted on a lonely bridge by some peasants who require her help in a superstitious ritual. Her assistance will enable a woman who has had the evil eye cast on her to give birth to her child. Sabel complies, and they show their gratitude by giving her shelter. Don Juan Manuel has given his servant don Galán—who occupies the position of jester or buffoon—orders to seek and find his goddaughter's hideout. In time don Galán comes across Sabel and she, in despair, attempts suicide by drowning. Sabel is rescued and doña María determines to protect her. She enters her husband's house to find him at supper. Embarrassed by the presence of his wife, he forces his mistress to go under the table. Doña María, who is disgusted by his crudities and insensitivity, orders him and Liberata out of the house until such a time as Sabel is strong enough to leave with her. Don Juan Manuel complies and at this point the play comes to a rather tame end.

This is, in my opinion, the weakest of *The Vandals* plays. It is the longest, the most undisciplined, and certainly the hardest to stage owing to its rambling and episodic nature. The essential point, however, is that it is not intended necessarily to be staged, but is seen instead as a narrative mainly in dialogue[13] which relates to the decline of the Galician squirearchy. *The Eagle Scutcheon* shares some of the characteristics of the two other plays. As one can gather from the summary, it is as highly colored as *Silver Face* if not more so; there is the same irreverence towards the dead, particularly in the body-snatching scene which is pure *grand guignol* and not to be taken seriously. Furthermore, considerable emphasis is laid on the feudal nature of the Galician social system. The scene in which life at its most elemental is contrasted with a corpse bubbling in a pot has been described by one critic as "one of the most perfect and grandiose examples of Valle's orchestrations of the macabre and the grotesque."[14] Certainly, it is virtually impossible to visualize a more violent juxtaposition of warring elements.

c. Romance de lobos

This play is by any account one of Valle-Inclán's masterpieces. It has the grandeur, the pathos and the discipline lacking in the other plays of the trilogy. It has been compared to *King Lear* and, within limits, the comparison is apt. Like the aging King of Britain, don Juan Manuel is refused shelter by his own progeny and finds himself on a lonely strand accompanied only by a madman, a social outcast like himself.

As Valle-Inclán himself stated, the mockery of death and the irreverence towards the dead lead inevitably to the arrival of Death; it is at this point that *The Ballad of the Wolves* begins. The first scene of this play is a *Walpurgisnacht* with a Galician setting. According to Galician superstition, the arrival of death is heralded by the appearance of the *Santa Compaña* or souls of the departed who warn the condemned man that he must prepare to die. Riding home one night in a state of inebriation, don Juan Manuel sees the *Santa Compaña* with their attendant witches in the village graveyard. They speak to him of his sins and, with the approach of dawn, take their departure. The scene unfolds in the best Romantic tradition.

Having arrived home, don Juan Manuel is given a message by a sailor to the effect that his wife is very ill. He realizes that the *Santa Compaña* has appeared to announce her death, and resolves despite the stormy night to cross the water to her home. The boat capsizes, all those on board are drowned, but this only occurs after don Juan Manuel has been put ashore. Wandering in the darkness towards his wife's house, don Juan Manuel comes across a large beggar band and decides to take them with him to doña María's home to give them shelter and nourishment. He is conscious now more than ever before, because of death's imminence, of his own responsibility towards the very poor. However, when he arrives at the house, it is to discover that the granary has been emptied, for in the meanwhile the five sons have been up to their usual tricks. Farruquiño and Pedrito have desecrated the chapel by removing the sacred ornaments, and the other sons have made off with the produce given to the lady of the manor by her tenants. When don Juan Manuel enters the chapel with the chaplain, determined to see his wife's corpse, he is overcome by the stench of corruption. Such an unequivocal example of the tragic and grotesque end of all human life, together with his profound sense of guilt at the way he treated his wife, depress him utterly. He locks himself in doña María's bedroom, refuses nourishment or contact with others, and prepares to die. But the inmates will allow him no peace and, therefore, after giving his sons their patrimony—despite the abundant proof of their corrupt ways—he leaves the house.

One thing, however, is understood: the sons must shelter the beggars and keep the old retainers in their service, for they are the inheritors of the patriarchal system and its responsibilities. Don Juan Manuel takes shelter in a cave with the madman Fuso Negro. They are joined there by the widow and the children of one of the sailors drowned after don Juan Manuel had been put ashore. Subsequently the nobleman discovers that his sons have thrown the beggars and most of doña María's former servants out of the house. He resolves to force his sons to do their bounden duty by returning to the manor house with beggars and servants in train. At first they are refused entry, but finally the doors are opened to them. The sons jeer at their father, and Mauro, the second son, deals him a lethal blow. Then a leper, el Pobre de San Lázaro, attacks Mauro. As they struggle they fall into the flaming hearth while the beggars, who have acted throughout as a chorus, chant "He was our father." The four remaining sons mutter angrily "Now we are damned and will be plagued by lawsuits for twenty years."[15] On this dramatic note the play comes to its end.

Much of the action of *The Ballad of the Wolves* is highly symbolical. Don Juan Manuel is depicted here as the repentant sinner who acts as a true Christian. His sons represent egoism and corruption. Don Juan Manuel emerges in this play as a truly noble character, not because of his social standing, but thanks to his actions. The play concerns both material and spiritual death, for don Juan Manuel's sons are spiritually dead and this accounts for the decline of the race. They have inherited their father's bad qualities: violence, lustfulness, intransigence, but without his fundamental nobility of heart. Furthermore, the play shows Valle-Inclán's intense interest in the extremes of the social scale, something which explains why he could feel sympathy for both the Carlists and the Anarchists at one and the same time. What he never had time for at any point in his writing career was the middle class. Perhaps this is because the moderation and sobriety traditionally associated with this social stratum did not accord with his love of violent contrasts.

In effect this play could stand on its own as evidence of

Valle-Inclán's strongly rooted social beliefs. The other two plays contribute in their way to our knowledge of the Montenegro clan, but they lack the emotional intensity, the compactness and the depth of *The Ballad of the Wolves* which is undisputedly one of Valle's major artistic achievements.

II   *The Interim Period: the Farces*

After *The Vandals,* Valle-Inclán moves away from a regional and epic type of drama to one that is in sharp contrast to it; for the farces that belong to this interim period of Valle's writing career are lighthearted, delicate and witty in tone with back-cloths that are deliberately stylized and unreal. Valle-Inclán makes use of the techniques of dehumanization and also avails himself of *modernista* "props" such as swans which glide across shimmering lakes, frivolous aristocrats, and medieval minstrels. These farces form the bulk of the author's output from 1909 to 1917, a period when Valle appears to be in meditative mood and is rethinking his approach to literature.

It is not my intention to discuss all the farces in detail because their quality is uneven.[16] However, I shall list them all and comment on their most interesting features in passing. Both *Cuento de abril (April Story)* and *La cabeza del dragón (The Dragon's Head)* belong to the year 1909. The first is set in an idealized court in Provence in medieval times, and contrasts the pagan and Christian attitudes to love. *The Dragon's Head* purports to be a children's pantomime, but Valle makes use of this camouflage to direct some satirical shafts at the Royal Family, politicians, and empty-headed, pedantic scholars.[17] *Voces de gesta (Epic Voices)*, 1911, is the author's last piece of Carlist propaganda. It is set in medieval times with the Carlist Pretender thinly disguised as King Carlino who is being pursued by the wicked Moors. The symbolism is obvious, the verse grandil-oquent, and the characters hollow. It is, in short, a bad play. *La marquesa Rosalinda (Lady Rosalind)*, 1912, is perhaps the finest of all these farces. Once more Valle contrasts the pagan or sensual attitude to love, on this occasion as revealed in France, with the ascetic attitude of Castile. *El embrujado (A Man Bewitched)*, 1913, is exceptional among plays of this period because it is not an airy farce with an idealized setting. Instead, it concerns a grasping Galician squire determined to wrest his illegitimate grandchild from his mother, Rosa Galans, who resorts to witchcraft to thwart his plans. Like *Epic Voices,* it is by no means among the best plays written by Valle. But it is of interest in that it shows his undying interest in Galicia and its superstitions. It also shows that his idealized concept of the rural gentry is in process of revision, for Pedro Bolaño is not a sympathetic character.

The last farce in this group is the *Farsa de la enamorada del rey (Farce of the Maid who Loved a King),* which was published in 1917. This is a reworking of the traditional Autumn-Spring theme which seems to have exercised a certain fascination on Valle-Inclán. A young girl, the daughter of an innkeeper, falls in love with the aging king of the realm. Upon seeing him in the flesh her illusions crumble since he is ugly and decrepit and not the splendid youthful monarch she had conceived in her overfertile imagination. In terms of setting the author is deliberately recalling the *Quixote,*[18] although as one of the characters portrayed is Casanova, the action takes place in the eighteenth century. It seems likely that in this farce Valle is expressing his own disillusionment with the Carlist cause: "Rey Carlino," like the elderly king in *Farce of the Maid who Loved a King,* does not bear up to close scrutiny.

Something I have endeavored to stress in this study is the underlying unity of Valle-Inclán's production: a single preoccupation of the author can be traced in a variety of forms throughout his writing career. His strong opposition to the Castilian concept of "honor," particularly as it relates to womanly modesty and chastity, becomes an increasingly important factor in his work, and is already the principal theme of both *Lady Rosalind* (1912) and *April Story* (1909). The most virulent and impassioned attack on the concept of honor is to be found in *Don Friolera's Horns* (1921). In the earlier farces the author's point, although obvious enough, is yet treated with a fair measure of levity and detachment.

Lady Rosalind begins with a prologue given by Harlequin.[19] The prologue acts as a bridge between the world of reality and the totally unreal and frivolous one of farce. The action of the play takes place in the gardens of a Spanish manor house in the eighteenth century. Rosalind is a mature and still attractive aristocrat. She falls in love with Harlequin who leads a group of impoverished strolling players. They are offered shelter by Rosalind's husband, the Marquis D'Olbray. Rosalind talks to a friend, Amaranta, about her feelings for Harlequin. Amaranta expresses alarm at the Marquis' reactions, but Rosalind scoffs at this and says of him:

> Theologian of love, the friend of wordly clerics
> a gallant at Versailles, the page of the Sun King,
> The Marquis smiles at the absurdities
> and the husbands of the Spanish Theater.[20]

Rosalind then discovers that her elderly husband is no longer prepared to ignore her indiscretions. She becomes aware to her chagrin that he has been affected by the atmosphere of Castile and threatens to have her enclosed in a convent if she indulges in a clandestine relationship with Harlequin. He is no longer the complaisant, indulgent husband she had known at Versailles. Instead he has turned into the jealous, vindictive husband of Spanish Golden-Age drama who is determined to go to any lengths to safeguard his reputation. Thus Rosalind and Harlequin are forced to part. He is jailed, charged with dabbing in occult practices, while Rosalind is placed in a convent. When they next see each other Rosalind has undergone a complete change. She is no longer frivolous and mundane, and has repented of what she now considers to have been her sins. Her sole desire in life now is to return to the convent. Harlequin himself is not exactly broken-hearted, so they part quite cordially.

Evidently in a farce of this nature there are many complications, sub-plots and minor characters. There is a scholarly and worldly *abbé* who is happy to come to the assistance of a lady if she finds difficulty in composing a love letter. There is, in addition, a strict, upright duenna—the self-appointed guardian of womanly modesty—who admits to a sincere admiration for the works of the seventeenth-century playwright Pedro Calderón. It was Calderón above all others who was the apologist of Castilian "honor." The other *commedia dell'arte* figures, Pierrot, Colombine and Pulchinella also play their part in enlivening the proceedings.

The settings, like the characters, are extremely stylized and already there are hints of the grotesque dehumanization of

88 Ramón del Valle-Inclán

characters which was to become so important a feature of the *esperpentos*. Referring to the duenna, the author remarks: "The witch-like shadow of the duenna rises up/ an owl dreams on a cypress tree."[21] (In *Don Friolera's Horns,* the vicious old gossip doña Tadea Calderón is equated constantly with an owl.)

III   Farsa y licencia de la reina castiza (1919)

This play lies midway between the farces of the interim period and the *esperpentos.* Like the former it is written in verse and has a certain air of frivolity and levity. Like the latter it contains satire of the army; its central theme—the misrule of Isabel II (1833-1868)—is to be the subject of the two completed *Iberian Ring* novels. Lastly, it contains examples of dehumanization which are much more extreme than in the earlier farces.

The *Farce of the Castilian Queen* concerns the amorous intrigues of the promiscuous Queen and the complications arising out of them. A penniless student has obtained a love letter written by Isabel, and endeavors to blackmail her. What he demands for its return is nothing less than the archbishopric of Manila. The action hinges on the complications caused by this situation together with the plotting of the jealous King Consort to discover his wife *in flagrante.* Although the farce is lighthearted, Valle is obviously concerned about the frivolity, ignorance and stupidity of the Queen, her Consort and her advisers, together with the completely arbitrary way in which Isabel rules her people. The characteristics revealed by the Queen and her husband are precisely those which are to distinguish them also in the *Iberian Ring* novels. Isabel is a kindhearted but frivolous woman who is determined that nothing should prevent her from indulging her whims. For example, when the Lord Chamberlain warns her that questions may be asked in Congress about her indiscretions, her answer is quite simply "Congress can be dissolved."[22] Furthermore, if something is leaked to the press, censorship can be applied and all will be well.

The figure of the cowardly, braggardly army officer, already adumbrated in *The Dragon's Head,*[23] is developed here in the person of Tragatundas, the general renowned for his exploits in Morocco:

> With jingling spurs awaking echoes
> of so many legendary exploits in Morocco
> Don Tragatundas goes his way.[24]

Without a doubt, the general who is under attack here is Juan
Prim whom Valle was to castigate so unmercifully in the *Iberian
Ring* novels, for he seemed in the author's eyes to epitomize
everything he found most loathsome about the military.

There are in this play a number of grotesque animal images
applied to the characters,[25] but the most interesting feature of
the imagery is that in this farce both sun and moon are affected
by the illogicalities of human behavior. In their turn they participate in the farcical actions taking place around the Queen's
palace. The sun whirls through the firmament like a ball, whilst
the moon performs acrobatic leaps over the tops of the black
poplars. The appearance of the moon is totally grotesque:

> The moon puffs out its cheeks
> and its painted doll's face
> red with laughter, stands
> out above the line of poplars.[26]

Particularly because of its sordid treatment of certain themes,
such as eroticism—the Queen's affairs lack the delicacy and
sophistication of the relationship between Rosalind and Harlequin
—this play is the direct forerunner of the *esperpentos* which
are now to be considered.

CHAPTER 6

The Later Plays

I *The* Esperpento

THERE are only four published plays defined as *esperpentos*.[1]
Three of these, *Don Friolera's Horns*, *Las galas del difunto
(The Dead Man's Finery)* and *La hija del capitán (The Captain's
Daughter)*, were published in a single volume under the general
heading *Martes de carnaval (Shrove Tuesday)*.[2] The fourth,
omitted by some critics because it is said to lack certain of the
fundamental characteristics of the others,[3] is *Luces de bohemia
(Bohemian Lights)* which contains the definition of the *esperpento*. Other plays of the period are *Divinas palabras (Divine
Words)* of 1920, in which the spirit of the *esperpento* is transferred to a rural, Galician setting, and five extremely stark
one-act plays published under the rather lurid title of *Retablo
de la avaricia, la lujuria y la muerte (Dramas of Avarice, Lechery
and Death)*. In these playlets[4] Valle carries the techniques of dehumanization to unforeseen extremes. In two of them in particular, *Sacrilegio (Sacrilege)* and *Ligazón (The Blood Pact)*, the
characters are nothing more than one-dimensional shadows. In
all four the characters portrayed are elemental, brutal, cruel and
depraved; this suggests that Valle is reflecting the Gnostic belief
that all matter is by its very nature evil. All these plays, unlike
the *esperpentos,* have a rural setting. Except for *Bohemian Lights,*
the works I have mentioned have one thing in common: they
are examples of Expressionist drama. The Expressionists rejected
any attempt at psychological insight, seeking instead to reveal the
latent physiognomy of things, that is, their essence.[5] In seeking
to grasp the inner reality of a character, the aim of the Expressionists was similar to that of the Symbolists before them,
except that the former were not concerned with the gulf separat-

ing the world of essence from that of matter. Furthermore, there are marked differences of technique to be observed, for the Expressionists' vision was much more anarchical. In drama, for example, they employed types and caricatures, choosing exotic or abstract localities; while in narrative, dream sequences and interior monologue replaced realistic relationships and logical consistency. As I have already mentioned, the exception among these plays is *Bohemian Lights,* which bears little affinity to Expressionist drama. In fact, in terms of his mature production, this is the closest Valle ever came to a "realistic" portrayal of human character. It is due to its differences from the remaining *esperpentos* that I shall consider it before the others.

II   Luces de bohemia (1920)

Bohemian Lights is that very rare phenomenon in Valle's production, a work in which the author's emotions, perhaps against his will, are very much in evidence. It is clear that he the author is filled with despair at the state of his own country and, like the protagonist Max Estrella, experiences bitter rage at his impotence: the individual, isolated in a largely Philistine society, can do little if anything to remedy the situation.

Like *The Eagle Scutcheon* this play is a rambling, episodic work which would fit better into the category of a novel in dialogue than a play. I shall attempt to give a résumé of the most important events. Max Estrella is a down-at-heel poet living with his French wife and a single daughter in complete penury. The cry set up by the essayist Mariano José de Larra almost one hundred years before, to the effect that there is no reading public in Spain is still applicable according to Valle-Inclán. There is no appreciation of talent and, as an Anarchist comments bitterly to Max when they share a cell, "In Spain work and intelligence have always been despised. Here everything is controlled by money."[6]

In the background there are social unrest and street rioting, for the events narrated are strictly contemporaneous, applying to the year 1920.[7] Max has a companion, don Latino de Hispalis, who follows him around like a faithful dog. Together they wander about the city calling first on a bookseller of their acquaintance and then joining some of their cronies in a tavern. After a night's hard drinking Max is clapped into prison for insulting behavior to the authorities. His cell companion turns out to be an Anarchist industrial worker from Barcelona. This is a most poignant scene, since it is obvious that despite his Traditionalist leanings Valle-Inclán feels much sympathy for the Anarchists and their ideal of a society free of the evils of the "Money God." The Anarchist, whom Max dubs Saul, knows that he is bound to be killed according to the then notorious *ley de fugas,* whereby the police shoot a prisoner in cold blood maintaining in their deposition that he died while trying to escape. This is what occurs at a later point in the action, when firing is heard in the distance and someone says that a prisoner was shot while seeking to run away.

After the night spent in prison Max is released thanks to the intervention of his friends who have alerted the editor of a newspaper. He in turn contacted the Minister of the Interior, a man Max had known quite well in their youth. After his release, Max insists on seeing him. In this scene Valle stresses the contrast between the kindhearted but effete politician[8] and the talented individual who finds himself in the humiliating position of having to accept charity from someone intellectually by far his inferior. But what Max describes as the "Dantesque circle" in which he is trapped continues to revolve. Accompanied once again by don Latino, Max is accosted by a couple of prostitutes. Again, one is given an example of the mathematical distortion of the *esperpento:*[9] the park in which they are approached is described as a "grotesque parody of the Gardens of Armida."[10] After this incident Max and his companion are faced with the tragic consequences of the street rioting. They come across a woman bearing in her arms a child who has been killed by a stray bullet.[11] Just to make matters worse, it is at this point that the Anarchist is shot. Max seethes with impotent fury: "I am dying of rage. . . . Our life is a Dantesque circle. . . . I am dying of hunger, satisfied that I haven't carried one single candle in this tragic carnival procession."[12] Now, as at the start of the play, Max threatens suicide, for he sees no other way out. However, fate decrees otherwise. After don Latino has left him at home, Max dies on the doorstep.

After this there is a grotesque scene in which just before the corpse is taken to the cemetery, a Russian Anarchist maintains that Max is not really dead but is only suffering from catalepsy. This is followed by a very moving scene in the cemetery which

deliberately recalls the graveyard scene in *Hamlet*. It consists of
a meditation on death between Rubén Darío and the Marquis
of Bradomín. Here the Christian and Hellenic atitudes toward
death are contrasted. Darío fears death and refers to it as "She."
By ways of contrast, Bradomín considers that it is death and not
life which is divine, adding with his habitual nonchalance that
he hopes to be eternal on account of his sins. Later they come
across two gravediggers and the conversation that ensues is
tinged with irony. Bradomín asks at one point if they have ever
come across an inconsolable widow. "No," is the laconic reply,
"but one may well exist."[13] The play ends with the suicide of
Max's widow, Madame Collet, and their daughter Claudinita.
There is irony in the fact that a lottery ticket bought by Max has
turned out to be a winner.

One of the many points emphasized by the author in this play
is the indifference of people to the death of others: as one of the
characters says in the course of the action, parodying the famous
lines of Espronceda's "Canto a Teresa," "Only the undertaker
cares if there is one more corpse in the world."[14] Max, the blind
poet, is the *esperpento*'s answer to Homer, for one important
aspect of the genre is that each example should contain the
debased, modern version of a legendary hero. Thus Friolera in
Don Friolera's Horns is a puny, effete Othello, and Juanito
Ventolera in *The Dead Man's Finery* is a parody of Zorrilla's
don Juan Tenorio. These characters are in direct contrast to don
Juan Manuel Montenegro; whereas he had grandeur and mag-
nanimity, the protagonists of the *esperpento* are at the mercy of
their circumstances. *Bohemian Lights* betrays the author's nos-
talgia for the bohemian *modernista* circle of his youth. We recall
that the character of Max Estrella is based on the writer Alejandro Sawa, a colorful figure of the Spanish literary world in the
early years of the century who died in extreme poverty. Bradomín
is Valle himself; the eccentric Dorio de Gadex is another writer
of the period, Ciro Bayo, and Rubén Darío, the acknowledged
leader of the group, appears undisguised. It is the strong autobiographical element which accounts, in my opinion, for the
author's emotions being so much in evidence.

In *Bohemian Lights* many broadsides are directed at the incompetence of the government, at social inequality and at the
parody of true religion which is accepted by most Spaniards.

Dorio de Gadex, who has just returned from the Protestant atmosphere of England, has strong views on this subject. And Max, in conversation with him, states that "Spain's conception of religion is close to that of a Central African tribe."[15] *Bohemian Lights* gives one not only the definition of a new esthetic, but shows the reader in very concrete form precisely why Valle had considered it necessary to invent a new genre. Never again was he to allow his anger and indignation such free rein in a work; for this in itself contravenes the spirit of the *esperpento*.

III   Divinas palabras (1920)

This play is the *esperpento*'s jeering retort to the idealized vision of Galicia found in the poems of *Aromas of Legend* and in the novel *Saintly Flower*. The story is simple enough. Juana la Reina, a peasant woman with an idiot child, collapses at the roadside as the result of the ravages of venereal disease. Once she has died, her sister and sister-in-law hasten to lay claim to the monster child because, as they are well aware, his mother found him a useful source of revenue by appealing to people's charitable impulses. Mari-Gaila, married to the weak-kneed sacristan Pedro Gailo, is one of the contestants. The wily Rosa la Tatula, Pedro's sister, is her rival. Finally the mayor is called upon to pronounce a verdict and, like Solomon, he declares that they should divide the child: one relative is to look after him for part of the week and the other for the remaining time.

This is precisely the excuse needed by the voluptuous Mari-Gaila to leave her husband and seek adventure as she begs on the roadways and in the villages of the district. She soon forms a liaison with a dubious individual who goes by the name of Séptimo Miau. On one occasion when they are making love, the child is left in the care of a tavern keeper. She and her patrons amuse themselves, as is the habit of all concerned, by giving the child strong drink, enjoying his eager expectation and incoherent babble as the bottle is placed within his reach. On this occasion the dose proves excessive and the child dies. Mari-Gaila, affected by guilt, decides that she will ask her daughter to leave the corpse outside her sister-in-law's home. There is a nightmarish sequence as she returns to her house, for she is waylaid by the *macho cabrío*, the malevolent, lascivious devil of Galician legends. This scene is a symbolic representation of her own sordid relationship with Séptimo Miau. The child's corpse is left by Mari-Gaila's daughter outside Rosa la Tatula's home, but before he is discovered at daybreak his face has been eaten by pigs.

Rosa la Tatula determines to seek revenge and tells her brother that he should look to his reputation. Pedro, who has no strength of character, is the cuckold forced by social pressures to take action which is distasteful to him. To console himself in this unhappy situation he gets very drunk and then seeks to make love to his daughter Simoniña, thus revenging himself for his wife's adultery.

On one occasion when Séptimo Miau and Mari-Gaila have met in the country, they are observed in the distance by some farm laborers who start to give chase. Séptimo Miau escapes, but Mari-Gaila is trapped and the men threaten to rape her since she is in any case so free with her charms. Mari-Gaila prevents them from taking this action by consenting to be led back to the village standing naked in a haycart. This is duly done amid the lascivious cries of the peasants. When they reach the village, Pedro comes forward to take his wife's hand and lead her as a penitent to the church. The assembled villagers are about to stone the adulteress when Pedro Gailo intones in Latin the "divine words," "Let him who is without sin cast the first stone." The primitive spirit of the villagers is stirred by the Latin sentence and Mari-Gaila is allowed to go her way in peace.

As I have already indicated, Valle has no time for subtlety or innuendo, and the substance of *Divine Words* gives ample proof of this fact. The author is a master of exaggeration, distortion and violence. His best work is written in a major key with a complete disregard for moderation and "good form." The rural microcosm portrayed in *Divine Words* is debased and corrupt. Its inhabitants are motivated by greed, lechery, envy, or cowardice. The symbol of their depraved nature is the deformed idiot child spawned by one of their number. Yet Valle shows that even these monstrous human beings can be touched by the magic power of something beyond their ken.

A critic has pointed out that in the later phase of his production Valle often recalls incidents from his earlier works so as to parody his earlier, decadent excesses.[16] There is an example of this in *Divine Words* in the grotesque scene involving the maudlin

Pedro Gailo and his daughter Simoniña. This is an ironic comment on Valle's condonation of incest in the *Winter Sonata* when
the cynical Marquis, like Casanova before him, deplores the fact
that fathers are not allowed to satisfy their daughters in every
possible way.

Whereas the characters in this play retain at least one virtuous
instinct, that is, they can be moved by an appeal to the spirit, in
Valle's final depiction of rural life found in the *Dramas of
Avarice, Lechery and Death*, they have become totally inhuman,
evil automata. This shows that as he grew older the author's
vision of mankind grew progressively more pessimistic.

One final point I should like to establish about this play is
that it sheds considerable light on Valle's attitude to the cuckold
and the adulteress. *Divine Words* is diametrically opposed to the
Castilian code governing a man's reputation. Here the adulteress
emerges unscathed, and Valle shows how a married man may be
forced into action by others and not of his own volition. Precisely
the same point is to be made in the *esperpento Don Friolera's
Horns*.

IV   Martes de carnaval (1930)

Of the three plays in this volume, by far the most interesting
and artistically ambitious is *Don Friolera's Horns*, while the
last to be written, *The Captain's Daughter* (1927) deserves little
attention. It is an inferior work arising out of a particular political
scandal which happened to anger the author. *The Dead Man's
Finery* is a more absorbing play because it shows Valle's indignation at the gross misconduct of the Cuban campaign during
the Spanish-American war.[17] Furthermore, by parodying the don
Juan Tenorio of the playwright Zorrilla,[18] he provides us with
the debased *esperpento* vision of the irresistible lover who, in
this case, is an emaciated soldier just returned from the Cuban
campaign. The *esperpento's* answer to Don Juan's aristocratic
love is a prostitute.

V   Los cuernos de don Friolera (1921)

The structure of this *esperpento* is absorbing and complex,
bearing a certain resemblance to the poems in *The Marihuana
Pipe* entitled "*El crimen de Medinica*" ("*The Crime of Medinica*").
But in this *esperpento* we are given three versions of the same

theme, although one of them, as in "The Crime of Medinica," takes the form of a blind man's ballad. The play begins with a discussion on esthetics between two Basque intellectuals—obviously members of the '98 generation—who have decided to study their country by tramping its roads and byways. They are don Manolito and Valle's mouthpiece, don Estrafalario, whose name denotes something bizarre, outlandish or eccentric. Estrafalario maintains that what he seeks in his writing is remoteness from his subject. He would like to project a vision of the world as it is perceived "from the nether shore." Estrafalario also seeks to imitate a relative of his who, upon being asked what he would like to be, replied curtly, "Dead."[19] This takes us back to the third of the three positions which according to Valle-Inclán an author may assume in his relationship with the creatures of his imagination: the writer must be aloof, the god of his own creation. This is as important a feature of the *esperpento* as anything mentioned in *Bohemian Lights*.

The conversation of the two outlandish intellectuals is interrupted by the arrival of a puppeteer, Brother Fidel, and his dolls. He gives a performance of a lighthearted, traditional tale in which a puppet is soundly cuckolded by his wife. The husband promptly kills her but she comes back to life as pert as before. The intellectuals admire this flippant treatment of adultery, noting how remote it is from the "theatrical and African honor of Castile."[20] They both feel that the tradition to which this puppet play belongs is Portuguese or Catalonian or comes, perhaps, from the North of Spain. They then contrast Shakespeare with Calderón, considering that the former has warmth and humanity while the cruelty of Castilian Golden-Age drama is cold and dogmatic.[21] At this point the main part of the action begins. This concerns not puppets but characters of flesh and blood who are, however, doll-like in their actions and gestures.

The play opens with the introduction of don Friolera, an aging lieutenant in a small town on the South coast of Spain. An anonymous letter hinting that his wife, Loreta, is being unfaithful to him, abruptly shatters his peace of mind. Friolera knows that the military code demands that he should take immediate and drastic action: "Among Customs Guards there are no deceived husbands."[22] Unfortunately for him, the Spanish attitude is not the detached one cultivated by the French. Yet Friolera finds himself in a quandary, not only because he is a man of peace, but also because he lacks proof. It does not take him long to discover that the person responsible for the anonymous letter is their sanctimonious gossip of a neighbor, doña Tadea, whose surname, significantly, is none other than Calderón. In the meanwhile, three of Friolera's comrades have formed themselves into a self-appointed tribunal to pass judgment on him. The scene in which the three officers foregather to reach their momentous decision is a direct, vicious, and damning attack on the Spanish army. What Valle-Inclán underscores is the essential hypocrisy of these coarse and ignorant individuals who have the effrontery to condemn a man for a sin which is not his own, that is, supposing that it has even been committed. As the officers reminisce about their army experiences, one of them dwells lovingly on the native girls in a remote African colony to whom he was not averse once they had been given a bath and a change of clothes. But Valle does not rest content with satirizing the army, for the King, Alfonso XIII, also comes under fire. One of the officers, Cardona, points out that the King has all the military decorations although he has never seen action. Campero adds sagely: "He's been on maneuvers."[23]

The tribunal reaches its decision: Friolera must either resign or avenge his honor with a deed of blood. Friolera is duly informed of this and, while trying to shoot his wife—something he fails to accomplish—he kills his daughter instead. The third and final part of the play consists of a blind man's ballad which the two intellectuals overhear in prison. They have been incarcerated for casting the evil eye on a donkey. The ballad's theme is the story of don Friolera but it is a glamorized, popular and distorted version according to which the valiant officer kills his daughter, subsequently hacking to death his wife and her lover. Later he performs incredible deeds of daring in the North African campaigns of 1920 in which Spain was then involved.

Manolito and Estrafalario are in despair about this distorted version of the facts: "It's the infection, the foul infection that filters down from literature to the people."[24] They conclude that only Fidel's dolls can regenerate them. That is, only by a suppression of the outdated code of personal honor so deeply instilled in their people can Spain cease to be a gross deformation of European society.

In this *esperpento* the satire is two-pronged. It is aimed at the incompetence of the army officers while at the same time condemning the Castilian code concerning honor and reputation. The theme of honor and vengeance had become debased in its passage from Calderón to Echegaray and it now receives its deathblow at the hands of Valle-Inclán. Pachequín, Loreta's supposed paramour and the parody of the traditional lover (he is a middle-aged barber with a limp), recalls a line from one of Echegaray's plays, although he misquotes it: "Since the world proffers her to me, I'll take her."[25] Loreta herself speaks of her duty to her home and husband in terms which echo those of Echegaray's heroines when hard-pressed by some villainous seducer. The satire of Echegaray's plays is by no means new in Valle's work, and there is already a droll allusion to him in the early short story "Rosita."[26]

Valle-Inclán's satire of the three army officers, Cardona, Rovirosa and Campero, could not be more withering. In depicting them he makes the external appearance of a character a reflection of his spiritual make-up. This is an extremely common technique in Valle-Inclán's later works, one he may have borrowed from the nineteenth-century French physiognomist Lavater.[27] Rovirosa has a glass eye which falls out of its socket at a crucial point; Campero is said to be in the "cat group," while Cardona is said to belong in the "frog group."[28] Doña Tadea, the malicious gossip, is described on a number of occasions as a large, ugly bird or as an owl.[29] The latter is a fitting enough image since like this bird her victims are mainly active at night and she, like the owl, is a bird of prey.

Another technique used to dehumanize the characters in this play is to describe them as puppets. Friolera is visualized as "the puppet Othello," while his daughter Manolita has "the jaded air, the absurd sadness of those dolls banished to the attic."[30]

The satire of the army in this *esperpento* is not limited to the three army officers who form an impromptu tribunal. There is also a cruel vignette of Friolera's superior, Pancho Lamela, who, when Friolera bursts into his private quarters to describe his crime in lurid terms, is waxing emotional over a sentimental romance serialized in a newspaper. Being off duty, the worthy officer is wearing velvet slippers embroidered by his wife. When Friolera declares that there is blood on his hands, the Colonel's answer is that he fails to see any. His more perceptive wife adds hastily: "He's speaking figuratively, dear."[31]

Don Friolera's Horns is a very fine play. It is artistically effective in its use of a stylized construction to underscore the essential point of the play; it is thematically absorbing, witty, easy to stage and adds to our knowledge of the *esperpento* esthetic. This play is without doubt the outstanding example of the genre.

greed   desep

VI   Retablo de la avaricia, la lujuria y la muerte

It is my intention to consider in detail only two of the one-act plays written in the 1920's; these being *Ligazón (The Blood Pact)*, 1926, and *La rosa de papel (The Paper Rose)*, which belongs to 1924. However, I shall begin with a brief description of the most significant features of the two remaining playlets, *La cabeza del bautista (The Head of the Baptist)* and *Sacrilegio (Sacrilege)*, 1927.

The Head of the Baptist (1925), which recalls Oscar Wilde's *Salome*,[32] is described as a "melodrama for marionettes." It concerns a Spaniard, don Igi, who has made enough money in Latin-America to retire to his hometown where he has bought a tavern. His peace of mind is disturbed by the arrival of a youth—his wife's son by her first marriage—who attempts to blackmail him. It turns out that don Igi's wife died in rather suspicious circumstances, and since he stood to gain financially from her death he is considered culpable. With his mistress, La Pepona, don Igi plots to kill the young man while she distracts his attention. The young man arrives at night; as they embrace she signals to don Igi to plunge a knife into his back. He does so and the youth dies instantly. But La Pepona has experienced the healthy, instinctual attraction for someone who like herself is young, so she proceeds to curse don Igi roundly. The play ends with the tavern-keeper announcing that it would have been better for him to have showered his blackmailer with silver.

Sacrilege, subtitled a "dramatic interlude for shadow puppets," is a good deal starker than *The Head of the Baptist*. It shows Valle-Inclán's never-failing interest in emotional and physical violence. The characters involved figure also in the novel *La corte de los milagros (The Court of Miracles)*, published in the same year. The story concerns a group of bandits who are about to kill a deaf member of their group because he wants to abandon his companions. Before being murdered he requests a priest to hear his confession. Thus one of their number, aptly dubbed Father Veritas, shaves the crown of his head to form a tonsure. Then the prisoner is told that a Capuchin friar has chanced to pass by and is willing to hear his confession. As the deaf outlaw is blindfolded, he is taken in by this sacrilegious subterfuge and gives a full confession of his heinous crimes. The play ends abruptly with the deaf captive being shot by the captain of the brigands who says curtly "Unless I shut his mouth the rascal will win us all over."[33]

The Blood Pact, like *Sacrilege,* is described as a "dramatic interlude for shadow puppets"; but the shadowgraph technique is far more obvious here. The entire action takes place in darkness with the characters standing out as darker shadows in the surrounding gloom. Visually the effect is most striking, since to contrast with the darkness there is starlight, moonlight and other highly artistic effects of light.[34]

The action starts with an elderly procuress seeking to bribe a young girl with a necklace of seed pearls and corals, so that she will look with favor on her client. But the girl is adamant in her refusal despite all the persuasive arguments used by the old crone who, like the girl's mother and the girl herself, is a witch. Angered by the girl's refusal, the old woman threatens to speak to her mother, but the girl replies that without her consent she is helpless. Furthermore, she will sleep with a pair of scissors under her pillow in case the unwanted suitor should be introduced into her bedroom. Remaining on the doorstep of the roadside tavern, she is approached by a knife grinder. There follows a quick-witted dialogue with erotic undertones, after which the knife grinder says he will return. When he leaves the girl is rebuked by her mother for not accepting the rich suitor. She knows that if her daughter is amenable her own future is assured.

The knife grinder returns and the conversation is resumed. But this time the young girl expresses her feelings for him in more direct terms. When they are interrupted by her mother, the girl arranges to speak with him from her bedroom window. Once there the girl asks if he would like to possess her, adding

that he would be her first lover. But first she insists on a blood
pact: she will taste his blood and he hers. The knife grinder
discovers that the girl is a witch but remains unruffled. The
climax of the action takes place in complete silence and is
described in a long stage direction. A shadow approaches the
tavern door and is admitted. The girl crosses the window, her
scissors glinting; there is a confusion of shadows, after which four
arms lower a corpse from the window. The end is highly ambiguous because the identity of the corpse is not revealed. Is it
the knife-grinder or the wealthy suitor whom four hands lower
from the window? Valle, with his usual reluctance to play the
part of omniscient author, allows his audience to form its own
conclusions.

Artistically, *The Blood Pact* is highly successful, particularly
thanks to the exquisite effects of chiaroscuro. It is also very
theatrical and, unlike others of Valle's plays, it is obviously written to be performed rather than read. Valle-Inclán stresses the
archetypal nature of the characters by denying them proper
names. They appear as The Girl, The Mother, The Knife Grinder,
and so forth. García Lorca was later to use the same technique
in his rural tragedy *Blood Wedding. The Blood Pact* also shows
the author's undying interest in Galician superstitions. In this
case the young girl is psychic and is able to tell the knife grinder
precisely when he thought of her during his absence. The white
dogs, into which those who resort to magic can convert themselves, are twice mentioned in stage directions. Whereas in *The
Head of the Baptist* the natural attraction felt by La Pepona
for her lover's stepson is thwarted, here there is a possibility that
it may have triumphed. Perhaps it is the unnatural love, the instrument of avarice, that is rejected.

The Paper Rose is very different from *The Blood Pact* because
here the grotesque predominates while *The Blood Pact* is more
poetic in tone. Furthermore, the characters in this short play are
not dehumanized to the same degree as those in *The Blood Pact.
The Paper Rose* concerns a brutish village blacksmith, Simeón
Julepe, who fancies himself as a demagogue and political orator.
When the action starts his browbeaten wife, Floriana, is about to
die. By dint of determination she has managed to hoard a fair
sum of money. She tells her husband to fetch a priest and not to
dissipate her savings on drink. While the husband is out, some of

their neighbors arrive to console the wife. When he returns it is to discover that Floriana is dead and that he cannot locate the money. He at once suspects the neighbors and, in a state of drunken rage, aims a pistol at them. In a stage direction Valle writes: "He grasps it with the glee and fury of a villain in a silent movie."[35] At this crucial point one of the children explains that before she died Floriana hid the money in a scarf. Julepe's mood changes abruptly; he showers lavish praise on his dead wife and tells their three children to bid a last farewell to their mother, "that martyred rose." After the coffin has been brought in and Floriana's corpse decked out in her best clothes, Simeón enters with his own contribution: a crown of pansies with tinfoil leaves. He then launches into a drunken and platitudinous oration in praise of Floriana. Affected by the alcohol he has consumed, Simeón waxes maudlin and then sensual. He throws himself on the corpse to embrace it and as he does so a candle falls. The paper rose placed between the corpse's hands and the clothes draped on it catch fire. The last stage direction reads: "Simeón Julepe amid the flames, embracing the corpse, shouts hysterically. The group of women recoils gesticulating. The entire forge is lit up by the fire."[36]

The significance of the title is obvious enough since the rose had always been a symbol of eroticism for Valle-Inclán. This then is the tawdry rose of the *esperpento* period. It is evident not only from this one-act play but from remarks and episodes in a variety of his later works that debased popular taste exercised a morbid fascination on the author. In this play he satirizes not only the ignorant provincial demagogue, but also superficial sentimentality and the vulgarity of taste represented by the garish finery placed on the corpse. In this context there is a revealing stage direction which provides us with a detailed description of Floriana's appearance: "The corpse in the coffin edged with gold braid looks as desolate as a wax model. The flowered scarf molding her breasts, . . . her hands with the paper rose peeping through the white ruffles, the jarring patent leather of her boots, all these things produce a cruel and pathetic discord, perhaps an inaccessible esthetic category."[37] It is possibly this very esthetic category that Valle is seeking to evoke in these plays, for he wrests a peculiar beauty out of so much depravity and disharmony.

An interesting feature about *The Paper Rose* is that it contains a further parody of death—yet another set piece in Valle-Inclán's later works. Whereas in the *Sonatas* death is contemplated as a beautiful spectacle, it is now the province of cruel farce. Since these plays carry the techniques of dehumanization to their limits, they are by their very nature sterile and, should Valle have attempted the dramatic genre again, he would have been obliged to devise a new approach to the theater. Although the contrast between an early play like *The Waste Lands of the Soul* and a later one like *The Blood Pact* is quite staggering, a critic has rightly indicated that some of Valle's favorite themes reappear in the plays of the *esperpento* period, among them sacrilege, superstition, the macabre, and the mingling of the grotesque and the wretched.[38] Once again it is pertinent to observe the underlying unity of Valle-Inclán's production, as is illustrated by his adherence to certain attitudes, themes and devices.

CHAPTER 7

The Short Stories and Early Novels

I The Short Stories

VALLE-INCLÁN reached his maturity as a novelist rather late in life. Consequently his earliest short stories are of scant interest. At the same time, they cannot be dismissed as juvenilia since the first collection of six stories, *Femeninas* (*Feminine Cameos*), was published when he was twenty-nine years of age. The stories in this volume are "La generala" ("The General's Wife"), "Tula Varona," "La niña Chole" "La condesa de Cela" ("The Countess of Cela"), "Octavia Santino," and "Rosarito." As one might expect, these short stories reveal that Valle is experimenting with a number of styles, imitating various popular writers of the period, including the French author Barbey d'Aurevilly and, in addition, Rubén Darío. He seems as yet uncertain as to the form best suited to his own talents. Of these stories, whose quality is uneven, the most interesting for different reasons are "La niña Chole" and "Rosarito." The former is an adumbration of the more ambitious *Summer Sonata*, and shows that Valle's desire to shock the bourgeois by allusions to sadism and perversion arose only after he had written the earlier draft. For whereas in "La niña Chole" the beautiful Mexican woman is married to an Englishman—something which is no doubt meant to suggest the very acme of respectability—in the *Summer Sonata* she not only has a torrid love affair with Bradomín himself, but is also the mistress of her father, General Bermúdez.

"Rosarito" is the most mature of these stories and also the greatest artistic success, to such an extent that it does not harmonize with the others. In this story Valle uses what was to become a favorite juxtaposition of his *modernista* phase, that of the virginal adolescent versus the mature lecher. Rosarito is an innocent and lovely girl living with her grandmother the Countess of Cela at her Galician manor house. A peaceful evening is disrupted by the arrival of a relative who is very much the black sheep of the family. This is don Miguel de Montenegro who bears no relation to the later don Juan Manuel, for the former is a Liberal living in exile beyond the Portuguese frontier. Being in danger of arrest in Spain, he asks the Countess if she will give him shelter for the night. It is implied that don Miguel is something of a satanic hero, having been influenced by reading Byron in his youth. Certainly, he exercises an irresistible fascination for Rosarito, a fascination mixed with the instinctual recoil of a young girl from a prurient, mature man.

The story reaches a dramatic and unexpected climax which is a masterpiece of impressionistic writing. Here the author describes the grandmother's reactions as she wakes from a doze at midnight imagining that she has heard a shout in the distance. In the description that follows Valle tells of the various sensations and impressions the elderly woman experiences. She hears the ticking of a clock, then a large black cat—always an ill omen in Valle's works—challenges her with flashing eyes and lashing tail. Becoming progressively more alarmed, she approaches her granddaughter's room to find her stretched out on her bed with a gold pin piercing her breast. The window is open and the room full of shadows which appear to leap in nightmarish fashion from wall to ceiling and back. The most impressive coda to this story shows Valle's ability at this comparatively early stage to induce a strong sensation of fear in the reader by evocative writing which hints at danger and tragedy.

Corte de amor (Court of Love), published in 1903, contains four short stories: "Eulalia," "Rosita," "Beatriz," and "Augusta."[1] Like the earlier collection, *Feminine Cameos*, these stories are the province of womankind, although the frivolous and vicious coquettes of the first collection have given way in at least two of them, "Eulalia" and "Beatriz," to a rather different kind of woman. Augusta is in the same mold as the earlier heroines, but the "decadent" element is now more pronounced. This is shown by the fact that the mature and voluptuous Augusta determines to marry her lover, Attilio, to her daughter so that they may continue their relationship without arousing her husband's suspicion. Something Valle stresses here as in the *Summer*

Sonata is the fecundity and sensuality of nature which echoes the erotic theme of the story itself.

"Beatriz," a much finer story than "Augusta," is written in a very different vein.[2] It concerns the daughter of a Galician aristocrat seduced by a friar who is her mother's chaplain. The chaplain bewitches her and, to remove the spell, an old woman renowned in the district for her skill in magic is called in to give assistance. Thanks to her occult powers, Beatriz recovers; later the friar's corpse is found floating in a river.

These stories reveal by their great variety that there remains at this stage a certain disorientation on the author's part. Once Valle-Inclán began to feel secure about his literary aims, he abandoned the short story, dedicating himself to longer and more exacting works.

Most of Valle-Inclán's short stories with a Galician setting— "Rosarito" among them—were not published in a definitive edition until 1914, under the title of *Jardín umbrío (The Shaded Garden)*. The significant subtitle of this collection is "Stories of Saints, Lost Souls, Phantoms and Thieves." Nearly all these stories, except "Tragedia de ensueño" ("Dream Tragedy") and "Comedia de ensueño" ("Dream Comedy"), which show the influence of the Belgian dramatist Maeterlinck, reveal Valle's unflagging interest in the folklore of his own region. Some, like the exceptionally good "Mi hermana Antonia" ("My Sister Antonia") of 1909, or the earlier "Beatriz," are concerned with witchcraft and the exorcising of souls possessed by the devil; while others like "Mi bisabuelo" ("My Great-grandfather") or "Un cabecilla" ("A Chieftain") reveal Valle's Traditionalist leanings. "Nochebuena" ("Christmas Eve") resembles the poems of *Aromas of Legend* in that it includes Galician traditional songs, and "La adoración de los reyes" ("The Adoration of the Wise Men") is a popular Galician interpretation of the story of the Magi in which the events are transferred to a local setting. A number of these stories were published either in newspapers or in book form before the definitive edition of 1914. As is the case also with the stories included in *Court of Love,* Valle has been reproached for republishing the same material in different collections. The reason adduced by one critic is that the author lacked invention. In my opinion the principal reason is somewhat more prosaic:

Valle needed the money to be obtained from publishing works
of fiction.

II   The Sonatas

The titles of the four novels are in themselves significant in
two distinct ways. Firstly, they reveal the interest among writers
of the period in equating literature with music; secondly, each
season of the year is taken as a symbol of a particular age in a
man's life and is given an appropriate setting. In these works
Valle is primarily concerned neither with relating a straightforward story nor with provoking an intellectual response; instead
he is seeking by impressionistic writing to arouse a whole sequence of strong and agreeable sensations.

The protagonist of the *Sonatas* is the ubiquitous Xavier de
Bradomín, a Galician Marquis with a pronounced weakness for
women. Bradomín is a composite character, aspects of him
having been borrowed from a number of sources. He is, for
example, the quintessence of the decadent hero, owing something to Nietzsche's Overman, to Des Esseintes in Huysmans' *A
Rebours* and a good deal also to Baudelaire's personal conception
of the dandy. Valle-Inclán was to say later in life when speaking
of these novels that they were "literature fashioned from literature," and the remark is equally applicable to their protagonist.

Bradomín is also something of a fantasy projection on Valle-
Inclán's part, for it is obvious that the amputation of Bradomín's
arm in the *Winter Sonata* recalls the amputation of the author's
left arm in much more prosaic circumstances. In Valle's later
works, such as the *Iberian Ring* and the play *Bohemian Lights,*
Bradomín was to figure quite unmistakably as the author's
alter ego. The writer describes Bradomín as "an ugly, sentimental,
Catholic Don Juan." But this definition should not be accepted
at face value, as it should be borne in mind that throughout these
novels Valle-Inclán has his tongue in his cheek: not only is
Bradomín himself a detached, impassive individual; the author
in his turn is not involved with his creation. When considering
the three Don Juan figures in Valle's production, Díaz-Plaja
classifies Bradomín as the ironic Don Juan.[3] Certainly, there
is much evidence to support this opinion, as a closer study will
show.

The style of the *Sonatas* is elaborate and polished. Valle-

Inclán draws on any number of the resources favored by the *modernistas* to make his prose musical and sensuous. He uses archaisms, snatches of Galician dialect, alliteration, verse metres, and tends to employ two or three adjectives with a single noun to produce an effect of balance and harmony. As I have already mentioned, Valle-Inclán was always conscious of the artistic value of light effects, and these are used with considerable skill in the *Sonatas*. He contrasts light and dark, refers often to flashes of light on windows, metals and jewels, and, to make the atmosphere nebulous and dreamlike, dwells on reflections in water and mirrors.

The atmosphere of the *Sonatas* is essentially aristocratic, esthetic values being paramount. Valle coldly ignores anything he considers ugly or which lacks a patent of nobility. The author also seeks to give these novels an archaic air, for although set in the nineteenth century—like the bulk of his work—the atmosphere evoked belongs to earlier historical periods: Mexico at the time of the Conquest, and Italy during the Renaissance. When dwelling on the *modernistas,* Pedro Salinas described their work as literature arising out of "museum day-dreams."[4] In this way he implies both that the *modernistas'* creations are themselves based on artistic models—something which as I have already observed is very applicable to the *Sonatas*—and also that they tend to lean rather heavily on cultural props. Such props are a pronounced feature of the *Sonatas,* in which there are constant allusions to art, particularly to Renaissance masters such as Titian, Raphael and Botticelli, and also to rich tapestries, hangings, goblets and exotic bric à brac. What applies to art applies equally to literature, since to titillate the reader's palate the author refers with frequency to pornographers such as Pietro Aretino and also to De Sade and Casanova.

These mannered works, with their brittle characters and artificial settings are, obviously, period pieces. At the same time they are not totally alien to a present-day reader, firstly because the prose style is quite exquisite and secondly because the author himself is fully conscious of the exaggerations in which he is indulging, regarding the whole as an elaborate game. This lends to the *Sonatas* a certain air of comedy and flippancy[5] which is very obvious to the reader once he has discovered that Valle-Inclán is not taking himself altogether seriously.

a. Sonata de primavera (1904)

This was the third of the four *Sonatas* to be published by
Valle-Inclán, but it refers, as the title indicates, to the earlier part
of the Marquis' fragmentary memoirs. At this time (the action
takes place around 1830), Xavier is an officer in the Pope's personal guard. His is dispatched on a mission to the ancient town of
Ligura to inform Monseigneur Gaetani, a distinguished bishop,
that he has just been given a cardinal's hat. However, when
Bradomín arrives, it is to discover that Gaetani is on his deathbed.
Before he expires the prelate confesses that he was guilty of ambi-
tion and pride, for he coveted the papacy. It is thus ironical that
an important step towards his goal should have been achieved
when it is just too late.

Bradomín is invited to stay with the prelate's sister-in-law,
Princess Gaetani. She has five daughters of varying ages, the
eldest of whom, María Rosario, is about to enter a convent.
Bradomín embarks at once on the seduction of María Rosario,
for her purity and the fact that she aspires to be a nun add
enormously to his relish of the situation. But after a time the
Princess becomes aware of his intentions and with her steward,
Polonio, she plots his downfall. Bradomín is first stabbed in the
palace gardens one night, and when the attempt on his life fails,
the Princess seeks to deprive him of his virility by resorting to
magic.[6] María Rosario hears of the plot and sends a friar to
Bradomín to warn him of her mother's scheme. Subsequently,
Bradomín is told that a message has arrived from Rome requiring
his presence there immediately. Bradomín discovers that both
his coachman and valet are incapacitated by drink after dining
with Polonio and considers it prudent to decline the latter's offer
to find him another coachman. The following day he sees María
Rosario as she is arranging roses in a vase. Following custom,
Bradomín begins an open flirtation with the girl, taking a cruel
advantage of her innocence. María Rosario finds his advances
deeply disturbing, and to thwart him she beckons her youngest
sister, María Nieves, to her side. After a while the child sits on
the window ledge, the window opens mysteriously, and María
Nieves falls to her death on the terrace steps below. María
Rosario is driven mad by the tragic occurrence and from then
on all she is ever heard to mumble is "It was Satan. It was Satan."

Throughout the novel, both directly from the remarks of other characters and indirectly also, there has been a stress on Bradomín's satanic makeup. More than one scene takes place in the darkened palace gardens where Bradomín is aware of the croaking toads which signify the presence of Satan. Furthermore, María Rosario is probably intended to represent the Virgin, with Bradomín standing for the Powers of Darkness. The stylized construction of the novel with the death of experience in the person of Monseigneur Gaetani at the start, paralleled by that of innocence (María Nieves) at the end, is somewhat too deliberate and neat to be effective.

Of all the *Sonatas* this is the one most heavily charged with artistic allusion. Perhaps this is because at the time of writing the author was not familiar with the background he was describing. As he was forced to rely more heavily on secondhand impressions, consequently the result is somewhat bookish. Valle's favorite juxtapositions of this period of his writing such as death and eroticism, religion versus satanism and prurience versus purity are very much to the fore. The spirit of the spring season, not apparent in the morbidity of the theme, is captured by the youth and grace of the Princess's five daughters and by frequent references to the gardens with their gushing fountains and the roses and lilacs which pervade the mansion with their fragrance.

b. Sonata de estío (1903)

Of the four *Sonatas,* it is in *Summer* that Valle's mockery of the *frisson nouveau*—a literary fashion already on the wane when Valle wrote these novels—is most apparent. Here Bradomín is definitely posing for an audience, standing back the better to contemplate and admire his cultivated individualism and amatory prowess.

Bradomín leaves London where he has been living since the end of the first Carlist war and embarks on the "Dalila" bound for Mexico. His object is to visit an estate owned by his family while at the same time recovering from a love affair with a woman boasting the name of Lilí. However, the truth of the matter is that Xavier is not overanxious to recover from his personal tragedy: "Certainly it is true," he says disarmingly, "that I was travelling to forget, but my affliction struck me as so novelesque that I couldn't bring myself to dismiss it from my mind."[7]

On reaching the port of San Juan de Tuxtlán, Bradomín disembarks and goes on an excursion to some ancient ruins. While there he sees Niña Chole for the first time and is attracted to her immediately because her smile reminds him of the faithless Lilí's. Before Bradomín reembarks he is attacked by an Indian in a solitary spot and, although armed only with a stick while his opponent has a lethal knife, he succeeds in driving him off. It so happens that Niña Chole embarks on the "Dalila" the following day and together they make the journey to Veracruz. Once in the harbor, Niña Chole persuades a Negro to dive into the water to kill a shark. The Negro demurs at first, pointing out that a school of sharks is at hand, but having secured a high enough sum from the Creole, he jumps into the water only to meet a gory death. Niña Chole sits next to Bradomín and carelessly tosses the prearranged sum into the sea. "Payment for Charon," she remarks flatly.

When they disembark at Veracruz, Niña Chole asks Bradomín if he happens to be travelling in the same direction. The roads are infested by bandits and the traveller is advised to seek safety in numbers. Although Bradomín's route is very different, he gallantly opts to escort her.

The first night is spent at a convent where the Abbess assumes that Bradomín and Niña Chole are man and wife. Needless to say, no attempt is made by them to correct this misconception. When Bradomín joins La Niña in her cell it is to find that she is disturbed by the tolling of the chapel bell announcing that someone is about to die. The tolling changes to the death knell and the timorous Mexican seeks refuge in Bradomín's arms, whereupon, in his words, they celebrate "seven copious sacrifices which we offered to the gods as the triumph of life."[8] The following morning they attend the funeral ceremony for the nun in the convent's chapel. The solemnities are disrupted by some of the men in their party attempting to lay their hands on a bandit, Juan de Guzmán, who has a price on his head. Admiring the vigor with which he defends himself against so many attackers, Bradomín springs to his assistance and the bandit is able to escape.

By this time Niña Chole has told Bradomín that he is risking the jealous wrath of her husband General Bermúdez. The Marquis, as is his wont, remains unperturbed but suggests that they return to the "Dalila" and continue their journey by sea to Grijalba. On leaving Grijalba, where the Creole has given Bradomín offense by showing interest in a homosexual Russian prince,[9] they are waylaid by the wrathful General Bermúdez. Niña Chole jumps off her horse and grovels before him imploring forgiveness. He carries her off, but not before crossing her face with a whip. Bradomín does not detain Bermúdez, respecting his dual rights as husband and father: "At no other time have I been so faithful to the motto 'Despise others and do not love yourself.'"

After a journey full of hardships, Bradomín reaches his estates to find that his steward, Brión, gives protection to some famous bandits known as the *plateados*. That night his sleep is disturbed by the sound of galloping hooves, shots and muffled voices. The following morning he is told that the outlaws had kidnapped a rich Creole but, having panicked, they abandoned her in the road. Brión, taking pity on her, brought her to the house. The woman, of course, is Niña Chole and the story ends with their reconciliation. This is the only *Sonata* that does not have a sad, conclusive end.

In the *Summer Sonata* Valle indulges in his usual proclivity for violent juxtapositions. Bradomín and La Niña first make love in a convent with a chapel bell tolling in the distance for the death of a nun. The nun's funeral the following morning is rudely disrupted by an outbreak of violence within the chapel itself and the death of two men who are left on the floor in a pool of blood. The author also dwells lovingly on two forms of sexual aberration: homosexuality and incest. But in *Summer* Valle is not solely concerned with emotional and physical violence, for he also establishes a contrast or juxtaposition of a very different kind; that between the glories of former times and their sad decline in the nineteenth century. The abbess of the convent is the author's mouthpiece in this context. She is a Galician by birth, a member of the noble family of the Andrades de Cela. As she reminisces with Bradomín, she remarks: "What a sad fate that of our noble houses and how distasteful is this age of ours. The enemies of tradition and religion are in power everywhere. It's the same story here as in Spain."[10] Valle also expresses his regret at the passing of an age through his attitude toward the outlaw with a price on his head, Juan de Guzmán. Were Guzmán to have lived in Spain's Golden Age his fate would have proved very different. For after years spent in the New World as a ruthless Conquistador he would have retired to Spain to found a noble family and to die a peaceful and honorable death. As is the case with don Juan Manuel Montenegro, Guzmán's qualities have no proper outlet in the nineteenth century.

The humor and levity of this *Sonata* strike the reader forcibly at more than one point. There is, of course, the droll remark I have already quoted in which Bradomín dwells on his reluctance to forget Lilí. Furthermore, when on board the "Dalila" he wears somber mourning and whenever a pretty face appears he adopts the pose of a mournful poet "who haunts graveyards with a melancholy, woebegone air."[11] Bradomín's encounter with the menacing Indian who attempts to rob him is treated in the same frivolous vein. As he is about to defend himself from his attacker, the fastidious Marquis notes that before grasping his stick he paused to adjust his pince-nez. The unruffled dandy must always have his priorities straight. Finally, when Bradomín decides to spring to Juan de Guzmán's aid in the convent chapel, he mentions that when he was attacked, he leaned casually against the church screen and fired his two pistols. A gap opened in his attackers' ranks and two of their number fell instantly to the ground. Bradomín himself remains "miraculously unharmed." It is touches of this sort which show that when Bradomín asserts in *Winter* that his only purpose in life has been to amuse, and his motto is "Long live the bagatelle," he is indicating something of great importance to a proper understanding of the *Sonatas*.

c. Sonata de otoño (1902)

This is the most contemplative of the four *Sonatas*. Most of its action is confined to the manor house and gardens of the Galician palace of Brandeso. Bradomín receives a letter from a former mistress, Concha, who is also his cousin, informing him that she is mortally ill with consumption and would like to see him once again before she dies. Bradomín answers her behest promptly and the sight of Concha confirms the melancholy tenor of her letter. She is pale and wan so that the comparison that springs to the mind of the sacrilegious narrator is with a Dolorosa. However, Concha's illness only serves to increase Bradomín's desire for her, more particularly as she is much upset by the

prospect of dying in mortal sin. Together they wander through
the palace recalling the carefree hours spent there in their childhood.[12]

At one point they are visited by Concha's uncle, don Juan
Manuel Montenegro, and a contrast is established between the
virile country squire who is brimming over with animal energy
and his bookish, skeptical nephew. Then Concha learns that her
two daughters are to visit her (Concha is estranged from her
husband) together with her cousin Isabel. One night when
Concha comes to wish Bradomín goodnight, he persuades her
to stay with him despite her resolve to remain chaste as she
wishes to confess herself the following morning. Concha dies in
Bradomín's arms whereupon, a prey to fear, he decides to alert
his cousin Isabel. When he enters Isabel's bedroom she mis-
interprets the purpose of his visit and tells him to keep silent or
"Concha may appear." Loath to humiliate Isabel by explaining
the true cause of his visit, Bradomín duly satisfies his cousin.
Then he returns to his own bedroom to carry Concha's corpse
back to hers. At one point Concha's long, beautiful hair becomes
entangled in a door knob and Bradomín is forced to pull it
brutally before it comes away. The following morning Concha's
daughters enter his bedroom asking Bradomín to kill a hawk
which is about to fall on some doves. Bradomín does so and the
young girls rush off to show their mother the dead bird. The
novel ends with their cries and laments upon discovering that
Concha is dead.

Autumn is usually considered, with good reason, to be the
finest of the four *Sonatas,* something which may be due in part
to Valle's familiarity with the setting he is describing. The note
of frivolity, so apparent in *Summer,* is not totally absent here—
the bedroom scene with Isabel bears witness to this—but it is
more contained. Inevitably we are faced with the same violent
contrasts and sacrilegious juxtapositions as in the other *Sonatas.*
Here the juxtaposed themes are eroticism and death, and religion
and eroticism. Bradomín's pleasure in his mistress is vastly increased by the fact that they are making love virtually on the
edge of her grave, and also be the remorse she suffers at the
thought of dying in mortal sin. The passage in which Valle
describes the room as it appears after Concha's death is reminis-

cent of the earlier "Rosarito." Here too Valle uses a series of
auditory and visual impressions to inspire fear in the reader.

Much is made in this novel of the aristocratic setting. But in
this, the *Sonata* of earliest composition, Valle does not appear
concerned with the decline of the Galician gentry, a subject
which was to preoccupy him increasingly in the following years.
Autumn Sonata betrays Valle's interest in Galician superstitions.
On his way to the palace of Brandeso, Bradomín is handed a
bunch of herbs by a simple country girl and told that if he
places them under Concha's pillow she will not die. Later
Bradomín admits that with a mixture of superstition and irony
he did as the girl bade him.

d. Sonata de invierno (1905)

As befits the symbolism of the winter season the background of
the novel is austere and somber. The fact that the author's concern here is with the second Carlist War shows that his interest
is veering from the cosmopolitan settings favored by the *modernistas* to a concentration on his native region at a time of upheaval
and profound social change.

Winter Sonata begins with Bradomín's arrival at the Pretender's headquarters in Estella, Navarre, disguised as a monk.
The Marquis has adopted the disguise so as to elude the redoubtable guerrilla leader Manuel Santa Cruz. The latter has
good cause to seek revenge on Bradomín, since it is rumored
that he was responsible for convincing the Carlist Pretender
that it would be politic for Santa Cruz to be shot. Bradomín
meets another warrior priest, Fray Ambrosio, who is trying
to raise enough funds to lead a group of soldiers into the field.
Unable to summon the courage to ask the Marquis for the
necessary sum, he tries to extract it by force. Bradomín counters
his challenge with spirit until he appreciates the reason for
Fray Ambrosio's surly tactics, after this he is happy to comply.
Bradomín sees the Pretender, Charles VII, and learns from him
that he is uneasy about the pressures being laid on him by
certain eminent churchmen. From the Pretender's wife, Margarita, he discovers that the King is surrounded by traitors. She
implores Bradomín to protect him. In the meanwhile, the Marquis
has noticed that one of doña Margarita's ladies-in-waiting, the
Duchess of Uclés, is none other than María Antonieta, a former

mistress of his. That night he meets her in private at her house and she reproaches Bradomín for not asking after their daughter. Xavier asks if she takes after her mother, to which the reply is "No, she is on the ugly side."

The following day Bradomín leaves Estella with the Pretender, but they return in secret that night as the latter has a rendezvous at María Antonieta's house. The evening is disrupted because María Antonieta's husband, Volfani, suffers a severe stroke. Later the Pretender asks Bradomín to carry out a mission for him. He is to go to a village called Orio where the parish priest has detained two Russian travellers. The Pretender feels that the atavistic priest may burn them as heretics unless prompt action is taken. On his way there, Bradomín and his escort are fired upon by government troops and his left arm is badly injured. He takes refuge in a convent where he is told his arm will have to amputated. Bradomín arouses the admiration of all concerned by his courage and impassive front during the operation. He is nursed back to health by a timid young girl who is a novitiate at the convent. It does not take long for Bradomín to suspect that this is none other than his daughter by María Antonieta. But this suspicion does not prevent him from trying to exercise his still powerful attractions on her, using his injury to extract a maximum of sympathy from his putative daughter.

Sor Simona, the Mother Superior, reproaches Bradomín for the unruliness of his troops, whereupon the Marquis delivers an atavistic peroration in praise of violence in war which has a Nietzschean ring. In time Sor Simona discovers through Maximina's own confession that she has become deeply infatuated with Bradomín; therefore she determines that he should leave the convent forthwith. When she faces Bradomín it is to discover that he realized Maximina was his daughter, and at this point the nun's anger and indignation know no bounds. Xavier leaves immediately, suspecting that Maximina has committed suicide.

Having made a full recovery in Estella, Bradomín bids a final farewell to María Antonieta. She refuses to abandon her husband who is now a helpless invalid. The farewell scene is very stylized and one critic has justly said that it resembles the final moments in a play before the curtain is rung down for the last time.[13]

The tone of *Winter Sonata* is much more melancholy and sober than that of the earlier *Sonatas*. True, the theme of incest makes

a last, tardy appearance and, in addition, when Bradomin writes
of his night of love with María Antonieta he shows the same
relish over detail as before and the same desire to display his
knowledge of erotica. But such incidents occupy a much less
prominent position here than in the previous *Sonatas,* for Valle's
main concern is no longer the amatory experiences of the Marquis but the progress of the war. Xavier feels that the end is to
be a sad one for the Traditionalists, and when he says that he
had always admired Carlism for "esthetic reasons" he can lavish
no higher praise on the cause, since the cult of beauty is closer
to Bradomín's heart than any other single thing.

Without a doubt the most interesting element of the *Sonatas*
is their protagonist who, as I have already mentioned, owes a
good deal to Baudelaire's conception of the dandy. According
to Baudelaire, the dandy is born at a time when the aristocracy
is on the wane. His principal qualities are pride, indifference to
others and impassivity: the dandy never reveals his innermost
feelings, for in this way he can only abase himself. The attraction
exercised by this singular dandy figure on Valle-Inclán is obvious
enough, for he too is concerned with a waning aristocracy. Bradomín, like a true dandy, is proud—not to say insufferably arrogant
—and he dwells continually on this quality which he considers
to be the most important in his nature. The Marquis is in essence
detached and never becomes emotionally entangled with any of
his mistresses. He may be lavish with superlatives, referring to
María Rosario in *Spring* as "the only love" of his life and to
Maximina in *Winter* as "the most beautiful love" of his life, but in
all these affairs he remains, as one critic has described him, "a
choreographer of love scenes."[14] Bradomín is far too concerned
with the effect he is having on others, marvelling at his own
facility for inventing elaborate lies or amazed by the seductive
powers of his voice, to lose himself in another human being.
Thus Bradomín, here, as in the future novels in which he is to
appear briefly, is the incarnation of the doomed Galician nobility, the detached dandy who is forced to live during a period
which is alien and repugnant to him.

III   Flor de santidad (1904)

Saintly Flower is closer to a prose poem than to a novel. It is
an idealized evocation of a pseudo-archaic Galicia in which,

however, the country nobility only hover in the background. In this case, as in the later *Divine Words,* the stage is given over to the peasants and the beggars. Although the background cultivated by Valle is archaic—for he is dealing with the primitive peoples of the mountainous regions of Galicia—*Saintly Flower* is actually set in the nineteenth century.

Adega, the protagonist of the novel, is an orphan who lost both her parents in a terrible famine, *el año del hambre,* which struck Galicia in the early 1850's. The girl, then twelve years old, is given shelter by the owners of a wayside inn who prove hard taskmasters and treat her like a serf. She is extremely devout with the "somber, archaic piety common to the inhabitants of the rugged highlands,"[15] and has candid visions of Heaven in which the local Galician saints are given pride of place.

One day a pilgrim on his way to Santiago de Compostela asks the innkeeper if she will give him shelter. The harsh, uncharitable woman refuses, so the pilgrim lays a curse on her house. Adega then invites him to share the stable in which she spends her nights. The pilgrim seduces her and Adega makes no attempt to resist, believing that he is Jesus travelling through the land to see where charity is to be found. The following day one of the lambs in the flock Adega tends falls dead and the innkeeper fears that the pilgrim has cast the evil eye on the flock. So she and Adega visit the aging Saludador de Cela renowned in the district for his knowledge of magic. The old man suggests a remedy which Rosa Seeleman has described as "a vague synthesis of moon, tree and spring worship."[16] At midnight when there is a new moon they are to take the flock to drink at a spring overshadowed by an oak tree which must be at a crossroad. In this way the spell will be broken.

After a time the pilgrim returns and again asks Adega for shelter. He curses the people in the vicinity, considering them tightfisted and callous. As he leaves Adega notices that another lamb is on the point of dying; she weeps, knowing that Christ is avenging himself on uncharitable masters such as her own. When a traveller at the inn learns of the spell cast on the flock, he refers to his grandfather whose sheep had also been bewitched. The advice given to him was to throw the most feeble animal onto a fire. The first person to appear, attracted by the piteous bleating, would be the one responsible for the sickness of the flock. He should be appeased with a bushel of corn. The innkeeper and her son follow the traveller's recommendation, but when the pilgrim appears the son proceeds to murder him with a sickle· Adega realizes what has occurred and, horrified, she flees from her masters. Later she discovers the pilgrim's corpse and when she is joined by some peasant women, Adega insists that the mendicant was none other than Christ himself.

Adega, who now roams the countryside dependent on the charity of others to stay alive, prophesizes that she will bear a child born of her union with Christ the Lord. Sometimes the shepherds who give her food believe her, owing to their belief in miracles, apparitions and magical charms. After a time Adega meets an elderly woman who is taking her young grandchild to market in the hope of finding a good master for him. She suggests that the young girl should accompany them so that she too may find a new home. At the servants' market Adega learns that another menial is required at the Pazo de Brandeso —the name of the manor house in *Autumn Sonata*—and makes her way there. But it soon becomes evident to the other retainers that Adega is bewitched. Her sleep is disturbed by the nightmarish apparition of Satan seeking to share her bed. It is decided to take her to the shrine of Santa Baya de Cristamilde on the coast, where a special mass is held at midnight to exorcise the devil from possessed women. The scene at Santa Baya forms a lurid climax to the book which ends with a description of the possessed led to the edge of the sea, cursing and vilifying Santa Baya while they are immersed so that seven waves may wash over their naked bodies.

Saintly Flower is a hymn to nature with pantheistic undertones: "the voices of the young girls fused harmoniously with the murmur of the springs and the trees. It was like a hymn raised by all mankind in the great pattern of the universe."[17] The mystery of the universe and the interplay between its various elements is apparent to man whose eyes, as the author expresses it, "are open to miracles." What Valle is showing in this intensely lyrical work is precisely how thin is the veneer of Christianity overlying the pagan foundations of Galician religion. The Galician peasant is a Celt who has adopted the outward trappings of the Christian faith while retaining his belief in ancient legends

and superstitions. From the song of the cuckoo one can learn
how many years one has to live; from the magic book of St.
Ciprian, where fabulous treasures are hidden. The legendary
Moorish Queen who tempts the unwary with her wares may
appear to the traveller at any point; by tracing Solomon's circle,
the devil is banished; a shepherdess has visions of Heaven and
believes she is carrying the child of Jesus Christ. Although
Divine Words and *Saintly Flower* are in many ways in direct
conflict—particularly since in the earlier novel both characters
and settings are idealized—in both the author stresses the sim-
plicity of the peasants whose imagination has not been stunted
by dialectic. Adega's reaction to the Latin words murmured
by the abbot: "The liturgical Latin filled her with awe,"[18] is
equally applicable to the peasant mob in *Divine Words* when
they are about to stone Mari-Gaila.

Valle seeks to evoke indirectly the archaic and pastoral atmosphere of the legendary Golden Age. When writing to a
friend in 1904 about *Saintly Flower,* he said that it did not
resemble modern novels but was instead sometimes Homeric
and sometimes like the books of the Bible.[19] The novel has a
static air and resembles a pre-Raphaelite canvas both in its
stylized medieval setting and in the colors Valle emphasizes:
gold, blue and green. This archaic atmosphere is further enhanced by the use of such words and phrases as "patriarchal,"
"georgic," "age-old lichens," "venerable cypress trees" and "at the
manor house tradition reigns supreme." Although the peasants
dominate this novel, the feudal nature of Galician society is
implicit in it. Adega is received at Brandeso where the lady
of the manor is noted for her charity. Her servants too have
a pride of their own, for when Adega says she is prepared to
work for her keep, she is rebuked by the housekeeper who
points out that everyone at Brandeso earns money and receives
a new suit of clothes once a year.

It could be argued that here as in the *Sonatas* there is an
element of irreverence, but it seems to me this is not the case.
What Valle stresses when narrating the story of Adega is the
essential ingenuousness of the superstitious mountain folk. For
them, manifestations of the supernatural—be they in the form
of Christ or Satan—are not abstract symbols, but living sub-

stances whose appearance in their midst are to be wondered at
but accepted as fact.

IV   *The Carlist War trilogy* (1907-1909)

The three volumes comprising the Carlist War trilogy were
written concurrently with *Aguila de blasón (The Eagle Scutcheon)* and *Romance de lobos (Ballad of the Wolves)* at a time
when Valle was absorbed by the social problems of Galicia
and by active Carlist propaganda. The cosmopolitan phase of
the *Sonatas* gives way now to a regional one which, in the
later *esperpentos,* was to be succeeded in its turn by a profound
preoccupation with the state of the nation as a whole. Although
it is not my intention to dwell on these novels in much detail
since their interest is somewhat limited, I shall indicate briefly
some of their more significant features. Of the three novels, it
is the first, *Los cruzados da la causa (The Crusaders of the
Cause),* belonging to 1907, that contains most of the direct
Traditionalist propaganda. Unlike the two remaining novels,
El resplandor de la hoguera (The Bonfire's Glow) and *Gerifaltes
de antaño (Gerfalcons of Yore),* it is set in Galicia. At the time
of writing the first novel of the trilogy, Valle had not as yet
visited Navarre where much of the fighting had taken place in
the second Carlist war. However, in 1909 he visited the region,
speaking to a number of the veteran Carlist generals. He also
examined the battlefields, making long journey by car and, in
the remoter districts, on foot.[20] In *The Crusaders of the Cause*
Carlist ideology is voiced by three characters, the aging Bradomín, his uncle don Juan Manuel Montenegro, and the latter's
son Silver Face. Much of it is distasteful to the present-day
reader because it is posited on the conviction of the inherent
superiority of the nobility over all other social classes.

Inevitably, Valle shows his concern for the way in which the
new moneyed middle classes are acquiring the estates and
privileges which before the nineteenth century were the province
of the landed gentry. Bradomín's steward and his wife plan
to usurp the Marquis' estates by associating themselves with
the grasping moneylender, Ginero.[21] Don Juan Manuel has firm
ideas on the way to deal with such social upstarts. If he were
to raise a band of soldiers to fight in the war it would not be
to aid the Pretender but to raise gibbets along the roads to

mete out summary justice to "that crowd of clerks, bailiffs, those who made their fortune abroad, and those who buy the property of the nation. That mob of servants who are now becoming the masters."[22] But Bradomín points out that when Charles VII wins the war he will impose the justice desired by "we of noble rank and the common people who still know their place."[23]

Bradomín also muses on the fundamental error made by the Liberals: "The genius of noble blood . . . something that will always remain beyond the understanding of the Liberals who destroy all Spanish traditions. The country nobles shaped the history of the past and the same should be true of the future. . . . They were the only Spaniards able to cherish the story of their lineage, who venerated their forefathers and the four syllables of their surname. The people are degraded by abject poverty and the court nobility by adulation and privileges, but the rural nobility, the upright country squires were of the purest blood distilled in the filter of a thousand years and a hundred wars. And everything has been crushed by Attila's horse."[24]

Silver Face shows the same arrogance towards his social inferiors as his older relatives. Like them, the knowledge that his own social class is on the wane fills him with sadness: "The rural gentry is declining, the ancient families disappearing,"[25] he explains to Bradomín when he realizes that the usurer Ginero will probably be the next owner of Bradomín's mansion in Viana del Prior. The same consciousness of social superiority emerges in a discussion with Isabel de Bendaña, the abbess of a convent in the town.[26] The nun explains that she had given all her personal jewelry to a sacristan, Roquito, to raise a band of soldiers. Later, under torture, Roquito confessed that the nuns had rifles hidden in the convent. Silver Face reproaches her for giving a menial a position of authority. Before allowing him to leave, Roquito's tongue should have been pulled out: "With these common people you simply can't take enough precautions."[27]

Once again in this novel Bradomín extemporizes on the need for cruelty in war, echoing his fervent words to Sor Simona in the *Winter Sonata*: "In war," says the Marquis, "today's cruelty is tomorrow's clemency. Spain was powerful when she imposed a military morality which transcended compassion for women and children. At that time we had captains, saints and executioners, all a country needs to dominate the world."[28] This point of view is contrasted later with that of the nun, Isabel de Bendaña, who travels to Navarre to nurse the sick. In *The Bonfire's Glow,* the nun is stricken with horror at what she sees: "The war was beginning to resemble the long, sad struggle of someone about to die, a convulsive, painful grimace. . . ."[29]

Both *The Bonfire's Glow* and *Gerfalcons of Yore* are set in Navarre. Some of the characters appear in all three novels, although in *Gerfalcons of Yore* they are all overshadowed by the forbidding and austere figure of Manuel Santa Cruz. In *The Bonfire's Glow* Valle shows that Bradomín's fears about the course the war is taking are being confirmed. Earlier, in *The Crusaders of the Cause,* he had maintained in conversation with Silver Face that small skirmishes and isolated attacks were not the right tactics for the Carlists to adopt. He compares these sporadic outbreaks of violence to isolated bonfires—hence the title of the second novel—and what he thinks is required is one vast conflagration to scorch the whole land; in other words, the Carlist forces should be concentrated rather than scattered over a wide area.

The structure of *The Bonfire's Glow* echoes the fitful nature of the fighting between the Carlist bands and the Government forces. It is a rambling novel lacking the unity imposed on the third part of the trilogy by the dominant figure of Santa Cruz. In it Valle divides his attention between the Liberals and the Carlists; despite his Traditionalist leanings he does not depict the government forces as evil or corrupt. Certainly, we are given to understand that they are misled and that, unlike the Carlists, they are not fighting for strongly rooted beliefs but, rather, because they are accustomed to obey orders, know no better, or have no say in the matter. The novel ends with Roquito losing his eyesight after spending some time up a chimney while Government troops occupied the house in which he had temporarily sought refuge. Perhaps the incident in which the smoke from a small fire blinds the sacristan is intended as an ironic comment on the novel's title and on the course of the war in general: a small blaze will only damage the Carlist cause.

Gerfalcons of Yore is the most successful novel of the trilogy. It is dominated by the presence of the formidable guerrilla leader, Santa Cruz, whom Valle portrays with evident sympathy. This is the closest Valle-Inclán ever came to portraying a character in depth, although the treatment is not objective since the author's judgment is somewhat clouded by his admiration for the character depicted. From his very earliest short stories, Valle showed a marked interest in the character of the warrior priest who is prepared to fight for his beliefs on the field of battle as well as in the pulpit. In fact, the warrior priest is one of the more obvious archetypal figures in his work.[30] Here, in the portrayal of Santa Cruz, is the culmination of all his previous vignettes. The cruelty and savagery of this warrior priest towards his captives—and those he suspected of treason— became so notorious that after a time there arose a paradoxical and ironic situation. This involved both Liberals and Carlists pursuing Santa Cruz so as to put an end to his atrocities and anarchical behavior.

Valle, however, sees the character in another light. According to him Santa Cruz is a man to whom life is of scant value, it being this outlook which accounts for his apparently callous treatment of those enemies unlucky enough to fall into his hands: "He understood the truth about war and just how paltry a gift life proves to be. . . . Many times as he walked past blindfolded prisoners lined against a wall he looked at them surreptitiously and thought, as though paying them a tribute: 'Some day I too will fall with a few bullets through my chest,' And if his conscience troubled him at all he salved it with that thought."[31]

But although this is an apology for an inordinately cruel individual, Valle-Inclán does not gloss over the strain of mercilessness in his character. On the contrary, he gives us ample proof of it. After Santa Cruz has fallen on the town of Otaín he seeks revenge on a high-ranking lady of Liberal hue by having her tarred, feathered and led through the town on the back of a donkey. Not only is this a terrible affront to her dignity but, as she is elderly and frail, the punishment meted out is unnecessarily harsh and insensitive. Furthermore, Valle does not hide the fact that Santa Cruz is something of a megalomaniac, aspiring to lead all the guerrilla bands fighting for the Carlists. To this end he summons the other leaders to confer with him, but only one, a simple shepherd called Miquelo Egoscué, is foolhardy enough to answer his call. He pays for his lack of foresight by being murdered, whereupon the priest assumes command of Egoscué's troops.

One interesting feature about the trilogy as a whole is that it includes a number of characters who were to reappear years later in the novels of the *Iberian Ring*. In the latter Valle returns to a consideration of the same historical period. Apart from Bradomín, they include Eulalia Galián, Jorge Ordax and the mentally unstable Agila Redín. One wonders if other figures who appear in this trilogy would eventually have been incorporated into the later cycle of novels if Valle-Inclán had been able to continue it.

Taken as a whole, these novels are not the most successful or inspired of all those written by Valle-Inclán. This is not to say that they are devoid of interest, since they throw more light on the nature of his Carlism at the time, reveal his concern for the decline of the Galician squirearchy, and enclose one excellent portrayal of character in the figure of Manuel Santa Cruz. Furthermore, as I observed earlier,[32] the structure of *Gerfalcons of Yore*, like that of *Saintly Flower*, reveals that Valle became interested in the structure of the novel at a comparatively early date. But the interest is not sustained in these novels, thus causing the reader to suspect that, despite all his protestations of loyalty, his Carlism was tempered by the knowledge that there was no place for such an ideology in the modern world.

CHAPTER 8

The Later Novels

VALLE-INCLÁN'S later novels, *Tirano Banderas (The Ty-rant)*, *La corte de los milagros (The Court of Miracles)*, *Viva mi dueño (Hurrah for my Owner)* and the unfinished *Baza de espadas (Military Tricks)*, are without doubt the most complex, ambitious and rewarding of his prose works. The style Valle employs is taut and telegraphic. Furthermore, as I have already mentioned, he sometimes pares down descriptions to a bare minimum of words after the manner of a stage direction. This, however, does not mean that the later novels make for easy reading. Indeed, the reverse applies since Valle is as determined now as in his earlier *modernista* phase to enrich the Spanish language by every means available to him. When conventional linguistic resources are felt to be inadequate, Valle-Inclán offers words of his own coinage. Thus there are times when a dictionary is but an inadequate tool to clarify the meaning of certain passages. In addition, the *Iberian Ring* novels demand an extremely close acquaintance with the minutiae of Spanish nineteenth-century history if all the allusions are to be understood. From this point of view, it must be confessed that this cycle of historical novels is not easily exportable, unless a translation—a daunting task in itself—were to be made preceded by a lengthy introduction on the history of the period. It is now my purpose to consider these outstanding novels in some detail.

I   *Tirano Banderas* (1926)

This novel, undoubtedly the masterpiece of the *esperpento* period of the 1920's, takes place in an imaginary Latin-American state, Tierra Caliente, in the second half of the nineteenth century. The country is intended as a synthesis of all the states in the Southern continent which explains why its landscape, as

critics have noted, is composite and unreal. What applies to the
setting is true also of the language used by the inhabitants of
Tierra Caliente, for it was Valle's professed intention to combine
aspects of the Spanish language as it is spoken in various regions
of Latin-America. To this end he introduces colloquialisms and
slang terms from the River Plate countries, from Chile, Paraguay
and Bolivia. Because Valle-Inclán was better acquainted with
Mexico than with any other country in Latin-America, it is not
surprising that both geographically and linguistically Tierra
Caliente should have more in common with Mexico than with
other relevant countries; but Valle deliberately avoided identi-
fying Tierra Caliente with any specific land because the theme
of the novel—the downfall of a macabre dictator—is considered
relevant to the continent as a whole.

As I mentioned elsewhere, the events narrated in the prologue take place after those related in the body of the novel
and immediately precede the events forming the climax of the
novel contained in the epilogue. Much of the action related in
the central sections should be interpreted as occurring simultaneously. Furthermore, Valle is concerned with the depiction
of a social cross section and not with that of a handful of individuals. This is made abundantly clear when the author speaks of
his desire in this novel to imitate El Greco's technique of cram-
ming so many people onto the one canvas that it would take a
Byzantine mathematician to replace them in their correct positions should these be disturbed.[1]

In the prologue we learn that the Creole rancher who is leading the insurrection against the tyrant, Santos Banderas, is issuing
last-minute orders before the start of his march on the capital,
Santa Fe de Tierra Firme· In the first book of the novel the
reader is introduced to the dictator who has just returned from
a town called Zamalpoa where he has crushed an attempted
rising with his habitual savagery. Aware that revolution is still
in the offing, he speaks to one of the more influential businessmen in the Spanish community, suggesting that he and his col-
leagues give concrete evidence of their loyalty by raising money
that can be used to bribe the revolutionaries. The ultra-con-
servative régime of Tirano Banderas suits the Spaniards who
are able to exploit Indian labor and fear a change of govern-

ment because it may involve the emancipation of the native population together with agrarian reform.

In the meanwhile the tyrant has decided that one of his military commanders, Domiciano de la Gándara, must be arrested due to a small misdemeanor for which he is held responsible. An attempt is made to arrest him in a brothel but he manages to escape. Unfortunately, Nachito Veguillas—the tyrant's unofficial buffoon—and a student who had no part in the escape are incriminated also. They are taken to the redoubtable fortress prison of Santa Mónica from which political prisoners seldom escape with their lives. Domiciano seeks the help of an Indian, Zacarías, on whose loyalty he can depend, and asks to be taken to see Filomeno Cuevas. He gives Zacarías a ring as a token of gratitude for his help. Zacarías tells his wife to pawn the ring, but the tightfisted and thoroughly obnoxious Spanish pawnbroker, Quintín Pereda, aware that so humble a woman is unlikely to possess a valuable ring, informs the police of the matter. The police promptly arrest Zacarías' wife, forbidding her to take her child with her. The result is that the child is killed by pigs. When Zacarías returns home he realizes that Quintín Pereda is to blame for the tragedy. He takes his revenge by lassoing the pawnbroker and dragging his body over the cobblestones behind his horse.

In the meanwhile the tyrant is busy. He has asked his Chief of Police to discover if there is any scandal which could incriminate members of the diplomatic corps, as he fears their attitude may be noncommittal in the case of a revolution. His subordinate has discovered that the Spanish minister, Baron Benicarlés, is involved in a homosexual relationship with a former Andalusian bullfighter. The Spanish businessman, don Celes Galindo, is sent by Santos Banderas to warn the baron that should he defy the government the scandal will be made public.

A political demonstration organized by those in opposition to the tyrant is allowed to take place. This is because Tirano Banderas seeks to ingratiate himself with the revolutionaries so as to win them over to his side by bribery. Also, he does not lack patriotic feelings, and considers the foreigners intent on exploiting the country a far greater menace than his political opponents. However, the tyrant's supporters are scattered among the audience at the Harris Circus where the meeting is taking place. They, together with the Spaniards who favor Santos Banderas' régime, insure that the meeting ends in pandemonium with the police arresting two of the politicians who had spoken. These are the smooth, professional Sánchez Ocaña and the idealistic Roque Cepeda. They, like countless other political prisoners, are incarcerated in the fortress of Santa Mónica where the tyrant visits don Roque on the following day, offering apologies and making overtures of friendship. But don Roque will have none of it, saying that talking to Santos Banderas is like talking to "the serpent of Genesis."

Nachito Veguillas, seeking the tyrant's clemency, tells him that he was hypnotized by a prostitute called Lupita la Romántica. He maintains that she is psychic and was thus able to read his innermost thoughts and warn Domiciano that the police were about to arrest him. The tyrant decides to see the girl together with the charlatan who acts as her manager. He is given a demonstration of Lupita's powers as a medium, although Doctor Polaco tells him that, as he has not yet had the chance to develop her powers, these are limited to "the circle of the present." At this point the revolutionaries attack the town. Tirano Banderas tries to rally his troops, but despite the cruel measures taken to insure their cooperation he finds that they are deserting him. He proceeds to kill his insane daughter so that the insurgents will not lay their hands on her, and is subsequently shot when he appears at a window. The novel ends with a stark paragraph in which the author states that the tyrant's body was quartered and displayed in four major towns of the land.

The importance of the number three, considered in an earlier chapter, is carried over from the structure to the distribution of characters. Valle saw Latin-American society divided into three categories: the native, the Creole, and the foreigner. Each one of these categories is represented by three figures, the native by Santos Banderas himself, Zacarías and an anonymous Indian who is tortured at the tyrant's orders. The Creoles are represented by Filomeno Cuevas, Roque Cepeda and Sánchez Ocaña; the *gachupines* or Spaniards by the Spanish minister, the plump businessman Celes Galindo and the pawnbroker Quintín Pereda.[2]

Santos Banderas, whose name is not without significance as it suggests authority resting on religion and military force, is at the very center of this novel, affecting in arbitrary fashion the lives of everyone in the country he dominates. He is not an extrovert, sybaritic dictator with a love of fast living; instead, he is ascetic, choosing to reside in a former monastery, prudish, pedantic, and mentally unstable. The last point is emphasized not only by the insanity of his daughter but also by numerous references to his hypochondria and to the unhealthy delight he takes in humiliating those who like Nachito or Doctor Polaco have no defense against him. We are told too that contemplating the heavens through a telescope, as is his habit, served to "scatter his morbid thoughts." It is quite likely that when he visualized this figure Valle was bearing in mind such macabre dictators as Dr. Francia of Paraguay or Gabriel García Moreno of Ecuador who sought to turn the country into a theocracy by a reign of terror. The deadly nature of the tyrant's rule and the menace his presence implies to the citizens of Tierra Caliente are brought home to the reader not only by examples of his callousness and brutality, but also by the constant use of images to dehumanize him and equate him with death.

The first book, in which the tyrant is watching an Indian being tortured in the monastery's parade ground, is called, appropriately enough, "Ikon of the Tyrant." The reference to an ikon together with descriptions equating him with a wooden doll and a sacred crow is present to underline his quasi-godlike status in Tierra Caliente. Passages in which he is described as a mummy, or his head is visualized as a skull or a piece of parchment add to the notion of divinity that of death, in other words, a god bearing an affinity to the Aztec gods of pre-Columbian Mexico.

Death hovers also in the background: the action of the novel takes place during the religious festivals of All Saints and All Souls; references to the Monastery of San Martín de los Mostenses, where the tyrant has his headquarters, remind one that in the country it is impossible to escape from his control; buzzards wing across the skies of Tierra Caliente; the corpses of political prisoners thrown to the sharks bob on the water at the base of the prison fortress. Even the pottery fashioned by the natives is described as "funereal," adding to the impression that the novel is a symphony to death.

Of the three racial groups mentioned by Valle, those who are treated with least sympathy are the *gachupines* and other foreigners, whether the members of the diplomatic corps who are incapable of taking a firm line, or the rapacious businessmen and landowners. The latter group is intent on enriching itself by the exploitation of a typical "banana republic." Don Celes is a pompous, sycophantic fool; the Spanish minister, a homosexual and a drug addict who is sorrowfully aware that, in the intrigues of the diplomatic corps, Spain is given no part to play. Lastly, the avarice of the pawnbroker Quintín Pereda is deliberately overplayed to serve a dual purpose. The first is the straightforward one of showing how unpleasant the *gachupines* can be, but Valle also visualizes him as a caricature of the wicked usurer who is "grinding the faces of the poor."

The Creoles are more sympathetically portrayed, with the exception of Sánchez Ocaña who, as the professional politician, is equipped for action with grandiloquent speeches, empty rhetoric and wilting platitudes. A contrast is established between the two remaining Creoles; Filomeno Cuevas is essentially a man of action, while Roque Cepeda is a dreamer with a marked mystical bent. Filomeno has the qualities of an epic hero. He is courageous, upright and generous of heart. Circumstances rather than inclination have turned him into an ardent revolutionary, for, as he says to his wife, he could not in time have faced their children had he not taken action to end the tyranny of Santos Banderas.

Roque Cepeda sees the revolution as but the necessary first step in the emancipation of the Indian, whose position in the social scale is barely higher than a serf's. It is ironical that don Roque is opposed to Santos Banderas in this respect, since the tyrant is an Indian who doubts the capacities of his own kind, while Roque Cepeda is a Creole and has forsaken his social position to take up arms for the Indian. It is obvious that don Roque has been influenced by Gnostic doctrines, for when the author comments on his religious beliefs, he indicates that in Cepeda's eyes man is a celestial being condemned to live in a world ruled by Time: "Men are exiled angels: the perpetrators of a celestial crime, they seek forgiveness for their theological sin along the ways of time which are those of the world."[3]

The temperaments of the revolutionary leaders imply that Valle-Inclán was not overly optimistic about the political future of Tierra Caliente. Filomeno Cuevas is essentially a practical man who would be likely to retire from the scene as soon as his mission was accomplished; Roque Cepeda is too idealistic to compromise, placate and maneuver in the tough arena of politics, and Sánchez Ocaña's mind is as empty as his speeches imply. Thus it would seem that after a relatively short period the country would once more be the victim of a military coup followed by a further period of tyranny.

When elaborating this novel Valle drew material from two Mexican chronicles, *The Expedition of the River Marañón* and *A Factual Account of the Expedition to Omagua and Dorado*.[4] Both chronicles are concerned with the rebellion of a certain Lope de Aguirre against the Spanish king. Valle drew on the chronicles for the characters of Tirano Banderas, Filomeno Cuevas and Domiciano de la Gándara. The character and circumstances of Lope de Aguirre have much in common with those of Santos Banderas.

Both chronicles underline the diabolic nature of the tyrant Lope de Aguirre, while in *The Tyrant* the natives believe that the dictator is in league with the devil. Furthermore, the climax of the novel, involving the tyrant's downfall, is very similar to Lope de Aguirre's end, according to the chronicles. When the latter is attacked he is at first enraged and tries to keep control of his troops by cruel repressions. Then he decides to escape but, following the advice of those who are still loyal to him, he changes his mind. When only a handful of his followers are left, Lope de Aguirre decides to kill his daughter so that she will not fall into the hands of his enemies. Finally, he is shot by the insurgents and his body is quartered for the edification of the inhabitants. Valle indicates his debt to the chronicles by saying when Tirano Banderas kills his daughter: "according to a statement of the insurgents he knifed her fifteen times."[5]

The technical and stylistic excellence of *The Tyrant* is apparent not only in the elaborate structure and in the effects used to suggest simultaneity of action, but also in the exquisite descriptions which introduce and round off individual scenes together with the vivid imagery. The sentry posted in the monastery's belfry spears the moon with his bayonet; the stout don Celes enters a drawing room marring with his presence the gilded symmetry of mirrors and console tables. There is also evidence of Valle's interest in artistic movements, for on two occasions he refers to Cubism.[6] The techniques of dehumanization favored by Valle-Inclán in the *esperpento* period are much in evidence here. There is a variety of puppet metaphors including German automata, wire dolls and Chinese shadow puppets. Also apparent are certain techniques borrowed from the cinema, particularly in the episode concerning Domiciano de la Gándara's escape from the police. Here the cuts from the pursuers to the pursued have the lightning rapidity of a film sequence in which the technique of parallel cutting is being employed. One other detail which is very reminiscent of the movie is the description of a room as observed by the tyrant in a mirror.[7]

Both in terms of theme and style, *The Tyrant* is an outstanding example of Valle-Inclán's mature production. It reveals the underlying unity of his work in that the sympathy shown formerly for the Galician social outcast, the beggar, is replaced here by his sincere championing of the Indian's cause.

II   The *Iberian Ring* Novels

Valle-Inclán visualized this cycle of historical novels in terms of nine volumes divided into three series. These were to consist of a detailed interpretation of events in Spain from the downfall of Isabel II in 1868 to the advent of the Spanish American war of 1898. Unfortunately, the author was unable to fulfil his ambitious plan, leaving only two completed novels, *The Court of Miracles* and *Hurrah for My Owner,* a third incomplete volume entitled *Military Tricks* and, finally, some fragments of future novels of the cycle such as *Fin de un revolucionario (The End of a Revolutionary)* and *El trueno dorado (Gilded Youth).* It is no easy matter to summarize the plots of the *Iberian Ring* novels because of the number of characters involved and the wealth of circumstantial detail. Although they appear fragmentary, this is not in fact the case since, as I explained in an earlier chapter, both the completed novels of the cycle have a symmetrical structure which gives them unity despite the proliferation of characters and the variety of unrelated incidents. Valle seeks in the two novels to depict in breadth the social and political situation of Spain in 1868. It has been remarked by some critics, among them Pedro Salinas, that there is too much warmth and indignation in Valle-Inclán's blistering attacks on Isabeline Spain for him to be concerned with the past. It is thought, instead, that the nineteenth-century setting of these novels marks the author's intention to criticize the society of his own day. Certainly, the army is much under fire in these novels as in the *esperpentos* of *Shrove Tuesday*. Furthermore, one gathers from the contents of one *esperpento*, *The Captain's Daughter*, that Valle regarded King Alfonso XIII with as jaundiced an eye as either Isabel II or her puny Consort, Francis of Cádiz. Bearing in mind that the censorship during Primo de Rivera's dictatorship was severe, it is quite likely that Valle availed himself of this subterfuge to wage a full-scale attack on the political and military corruption of his own period.

In *The Court of Miracles* and *Hurrah for My Owner* Valle concerns himself with the monarchy, the Queen's ministers, the courtiers dancing attendance on Isabel, the army and various members of the middle classes, the proletariat and the peasantry, all of whom might be described as "extras" in a film of epic proportions. There is nothing amiss with the Queen, except that she lacks all those qualities which are either essential or desirable in a monarch. Valle's ideal of sovereignty is to be found at the start of *Winter Sonata*, when he describes the Pretender, Carlos, in church. Nothing could be further removed from this portrait than Isabel II of Spain. The Queen is a stout, tender-hearted, ignorant, sensual and weak-willed woman of the people who seeks relief from the constriction of her stays and the rigors of government in bonbons, maraschino, and a whole series of lovers. She utterly lacks the regal dignity and the imposing presence Valle admired in a monarch, this point being underscored by the various comparisons of her to a pouter pigeon. One very dangerous aspect of Isabel's character is that she is easily influenced by others, and is dependent for advice on a supposed miracle-working nun called Sor Patrocinio. The latter is in league with the party of the extreme Right, the Neo-Catholics. Such is the nun's influence on Isabel that cabinets rise and fall according to her instructions.

The caliber of Isabel's ministers is, predictably, very low. The members of the Queen's cabinet are described at one point as "seven puppets of very limited intelligence as is traditionally the case in Spain."[8] The only politician for whom Valle shows a certain respect is the Prime Minister, Narváez, on whom Isabel had grown to rely very heavily. His illness and death form the background of *The Court of Miracles*.

The army is lashed by Valle in *Military Tricks,* as is evident
from the title alone where Valle castigates army officers by
comparing them to the figures on a set of playing cards. However, although more space is devoted to their antics in this
novel, in *Hurrah for My Owner* a group of high-ranking officers
plan a revolt against Isabel because she has honored two of
their number to the exclusion of the rest. Here the author
speaks scathingly of their uniforms reeking of mothballs after
long periods of exile in a closet. This is because at the time
there were twice as many generals in the Spanish army as in
the larger French one, with the result that the ambitious army
officer looked for advancement in the arena of politics. In
1845 the Senate consisting of sixty-five members included forty
generals.[9]

a.   La corte de los milagros

The circular construction of this novel helps to impose order
on a work which contains a diversity of character and situation.
The first book, which is balanced by the last, focuses attention
on the royal palace, on the first signs of Narváez' mortal illness
which Isabel chooses to dismiss as she flirts with Adolfito Bonifaz,
a cynical young aristocrat who is to be her next lover. In the
last book Isabel is no longer optimistic or self-confident. Narváez,
on whom she had always relied so heavily, is now dead. This
means she is at the mercy of Sor Patrocinio who, by feigning a
miracle, contrives that the Queen should sign a list of promotions
which will cause trouble among the military. The results of her
action are related in the next novel of the cycle.

Books Two and Eight start and end in the salon of the Mar-
chioness of Torre Mellada, an aristocrat who is in the service
of Isabel's sister and rival to the throne, the Duchess of Montpensier. In the other sections of both books we are given an
insight into various aspects of Madrid life: clubs, cafés and
theaters.[10] In the second book, Adolfito Bonifaz and some
young bucks of his acquaintance throw a policeman out of a
window as a dare. The policeman dies, so it is felt that Adolfito
and his crony Gonzalón Torre Mellada should spend some time
in the country until the scandal has died down.

Books Three and Seven deal with train journeys; the first
with that of Adolfito and the Torre Mellada clan to the latter's

country estate, Los Carvajales, and the seventh with their return to Madrid. The violence and unrest of the city are echoed in the countryside where the landowners condone the activities of bandits who infest the area, counting on their support at election time. The journey to Andalusia is marred by the gratuitous shooting of a train jumper by the trigger-happy Civil Guards, whilst, as Adolfito and the effete Marquis of Torre Mellada travel to the station on their return journey to Madrid, they come across a corpse lying in the middle of the road. The Marquis is much upset by this incident but their driver says cryptically: "It's the same story all over Spain."[11]

Travelling with the two aristocrats on the Madrid train is a colonel who has just returned from Cuba. He speaks of the animosity in this island colony between the Army and the Church, something which parallels the situation in metropolitan Spain.

When, in Book Three, the Torre Melladas and their friends arrive at their estate they are greeted by the dying wife of their overseer. Her situation arouses only distaste and apprehension among the aristocrats, for they fear her ailment may be contagious. On the other hand, Torre Mellada is extremely concerned about the cough of his English thoroughbred mare, Fanny; the ironic contrast exemplifies the reversal of accepted values so typical of the *esperpento*. Tío Juanes' wife dies that very night; Carolina Torre Mellada, unable to come to terms with the grim reality of death, is driven well-nigh hysterical by the dogs howling in the distance and by a further ill omen, a bat which enters one of the rooms in the house.

Books Four and Six concern the bandits who also figure in the one-act play *Sacrilege*. They have kidnapped a youth, the son of rich parents, with the help of the miller's wife, her crippled husband and the overseer, Tío Juanes. The bandits threaten to kill the youth if his parents do not pay the costly reward promptly, but their plans are foiled by a violent storm which results in a flood. The Civil Guards capture the cripple. To prevent him from talking the other bandits lay an ambush as the culprit is being conveyed to prison. The kidnappers rely on the fact that the Civil Guards' first reaction when they sense trouble in the offing will be to shoot their prisoner, and this proves to be the case. It is the corpse of the cripple which so distresses the Marquis of Torre Mellada as he and Adolfito come upon it in the following book.

Book Five, at the novel's center, gives meaning to the whole by emphasizing its theme of death and corruption. It concerns the flood which devastates the countryside and the burial of a corpse. The body of the overseer's wife—who has died of cancer—has to be conveyed across a river on the end of a rope because the bridge has been destroyed. This delays the funeral; in the interval the corpse is placed in a field where its stench assails the nostrils of the mourners. Sounds, too, emphasize the theme of death, the action of the book being punctuated by the howling of dogs in the countryside. The scene in which the body is passed from one riverbank to the other is a typical example of Valle-Inclán's grotesque treatment of death in the *esperpento* period. The only parts of the corpse not under water are the waxen hands and the shoes. The moon, too, participates in this macabre scene and winks in the depths of the current.

b. Viva mi dueño

The circular construction of this novel is, if anything, even more pronounced than that of *The Court of Miracles,* for it starts and ends with the same sentence concerning the approach of the revolution which quipsters have dubbed *la Niña.* The opening book gives us an aerial view of all the centers where Spanish émigrés are conspiring against Isabel. The action moves rapidly through Lisbon, Paris, London, the Franco-Spanish frontier and, within Spain itself, the Montpensier's palace in Seville. In the final book the author employs the same technique of moving from one center of revolutionary activity to another, but here the pace is slower, for Valle-Inclán lingers over the meeting between the sardonic Bradomín and the old Carlist Pretender, don Juan. Xavier considers the latter a better choice for the throne than his son Carlos who has been educated by religious fanatics.

Books Two and Eight concern Madrid, its salons, cafés and theaters. They contain parallel incidents, since in Book Two the entire court rushes to the imported French light opera, *Los Bufos,* and in Book Eight the Queen and her entourage go to a bullfight. Furthermore, in Book Two Gonzalón Torre Mellada has a hemorrhage, and in Book Eight the Infanta's fiancé has an epileptic fit.

Books Three and Seven take place in the town of Córdoba. They concern the picaresque adventures of the Cuban Fernández Vallín who is acting as an agent for the revolutionaries. He takes refuge in the attic of a convent and in Book Seven is able to escape with the connivance of the authorities. Book Seven also involves the last of a long line of warrior priests in the person of El Vicario de los Verdes. Significantly enough he is by no means a Carlist. Disgusted by Adolfito Bonifaz' seduction of his niece, he decides to join the revolutionaries.

Books Four and Six concern the Queen and her court; their affairs occupy a less prominent position than in the previous novel. Now it is the various conspiracies aimed at deposing Isabel which form the outer circles of the novel. Book Four, like the first book of *The Court of Miracles,* describes the pomp and ceremonial of a royal occasion. In this instance the parliamentary session is abruptly suspended because of discontent among certain high-ranking army officers. The Queen's appointment of two new Captains General and her recognition of the illegitimate Count Blanc are to have serious repercussions in Book Six. In the later books Isabel appears vacillating and no longer able to command the situation. The dissident generals foregather and march through the streets of Madrid, but their show of force proves rather hollow as it is not backed up by armed revolt. Acting under the influence of Sor Patrocinio, the Queen signs her confession for the Pope and asks Count Blanc to convey it to His Holiness personally. Unfortunately for the Queen, the letter falls into the hands of one of the revolutionary parties, its scandalous contents providing excellent propaganda material against Isabel and her advisers.

The fifth book which, as in the case of *The Court of Miracles,* gives meaning to the whole, adds the theme of strife or discord to that of death. It takes place in the Andalusian town of Solana del Maestre where a fair is being held. The Marquis of Torre Mellada and his party attend a bullfight; during its course fighting breaks out between one of the gypsy clans and a certain Juan Caballero. The gypsies are out to settle old scores, for one of their kinsmen had been murdered by Juan Caballero thirty years previously. Juan Caballero believes that the incident which had taken place so many years before is being reenacted and that his adversary has been resuscitated with the aid of magic. This shows Valle's interest in the concept of cyclical time with its periodic repetition of all events. Adolfito Bonifaz joins the affray and is lightly wounded by a gypsy called El Zurdo Montoya. It is during his convalescence that he embarks on the seduction of the priest's niece, an enterprise that proves all too easy for the provincial girl is dazzled by his aristocratic air.

It is also while he is recovering that Adolfito instructs a Civil Guard to give El Zurdo the lesson he deserves. In the knowledge that the accomplishment of this task involves promotion, it is performed with such assiduity that the gypsy later dies in hospital as a result of the beating he has received. The book closes with the departure of some sheep stealers from the town under cover of darkness. The success of their illegal enterprise was insured by the outbreak of violence at the Solana Fair.

C. Baza de espadas

Military Tricks starts at the home of a financial wizard of the period, the Marquis of Salamanca. Adolfito Bonifaz visits him to discover how best to turn a royal mark of gratitude for his services into ready cash. Isabel has seen fit to appoint her former lover Governor of Manila. The Marquis' home acts as a center for one of the revolutionary groups conspiring against Isabel, and before Adolfito's departure a meeting is held to discuss the forthcoming uprising. In fact both the first and second books give us an insight into the various ramifications of the conspiracy in Cádiz. The second book, "La venta del enano" ("The Dwarf's Inn"), ends with the departure of the "Vulcan" to the Canaries. On board are some dissident generals who the government feels should be put into cold storage until the threat of a revolution has died down.

Book Three takes place on board a London-bound ship whose passengers include the eminent Russian Anarchist Michael Bakunin and some Spanish conspirators of the Republican party. The latter are being sent as emissaries to Juan Prim to ask for his participation in the projected uprising. The orthodox political attitudes and maneuvers of the Spanish are contrasted with the radical and unconventional political thinking of Bakunin; he points out to the Spaniards that the projected change of régime in Spain will have no fundamental effect whatsoever on the state of the nation. The third book also contains some novelesque incidents woven around the figures of a Madrid wastrel, his daughter and the latter's infatuation for the ascetic Anarchist, Fermín Salvochea. This is rather like a comic interlude in a Shakespearean drama, and is intended as a scathing comment on the debased, popular literature of the period.

The following book "Tratos belicosos" ("Bellicose Dealings"), takes place in England. The Republican emissary, Paul y Angulo, interviews Prim who consents to join in the conspiracy. Overtures are made by another politician, Sagasta, to the veteran Carlist general, Cabrera, and also to the young Carlist Pretender. The former refuses to cooperate, pleading old age and enfeebled health. Don Carlos, on the other hand, is busy preparing himself for a royal rôle: "The Pretender stiffened his bearing with the movement of a leading man rehearsing great rôles. As though in a mirror he displayed his dashing figure before History."[12]

In the last book of the unfinished novel, *Military Tricks*, Valle-Inclán uses the same technique as in the first and last books of *Hurrah for My Owner*. However, on this occasion the aerial survey is confined to the various foci of the conspiracy in the town of Cádiz. For various reasons, including the fact that both the admirals who were to play a leading part in the proceedings and the all-important figure of Prim suffer from cold feet at the last minute, the August revolt is a failure. It is at this point that the novel comes to an abrupt end.

As I have already mentioned, apart from the three novels examined above, there are also fragments which were intended to form part of future novels of the cycle. Unfortunately, space does not permit of their inclusion in this analysis, but it should not be forgotten that they shed interesting light on the genesis of the cycle.

It is worth considering the two completed volumes of the cycle simultaneously, since they are linked not only structurally but also thematically by the author's concentration on the Queen, her courtiers, and their dubious or nefarious activities. In the third book of *Military Tricks* the revolutionaries, whose position had already been more prominent in *Hurrah for My*

Owner, completely dominate the scene and no space at all in the novel—which admittedly is incomplete—is allotted to the Queen.

Speaking of the *esperpento,* Ramiro de Maeztu observed that it was "the negative aspect of the world, a dance seen by the deaf, religion examined by a skeptic . . ."[13] Certainly, this statement is applicable to the *Iberian Ring* novels whose devastating satire is of a totally negative order. Very little in this bleak panorama meets with the author's approval; when he does show sympathy for some of the characters, as is the case with Adolfito Bonafaz' charming sister and her elderly suitor Bradomín, the note that is struck is so unusual that it appears incongruous and out of harmony with the whole. Gone are the bold, upright country nobles of the Galician trilogies. They are replaced by the fatuous, sycophantic court aristocrats don Juan Manuel Montenegro had derided in *The Crusaders of the Cause.*[14] These city aristocrats are fundamentally ignorant and superficial; they are versed in nothing more profound than court intrigue and the sleight of hand most likely to improve their position in the eyes of the monarch. It might be thought that in his depiction of the Queen, her ministers and the aristocrats, Valle is guilty of exaggeration. But two critics, one alluding to the period in general, and the second to Adolfito Bonifaz in particular,[15] have noted that the *esperpento* spirit is present in the chronicles of the period. Thus Valle had little need to distort, for he chose a period which was by its very nature a parody of an equitable society.

It is above all Valle's intense dislike of the army which reveals that he is not solely concerned with a portrayal of the past in these novels. There are times when his comments are so acrimonious that they cease to be witty. At such times the author's normally impassive front, the "lofty vision" he sought to cultivate in his novels, is not in evidence, and the author speaks clearly with his own voice. By and large these are dramatic novels in which the author allows the characters to speak for themselves; but there is one extremely important passage in *Hurrah for My Owner,* reflective in tone, where the author gives his opinion on the course Spanish history had taken in the nineteenth century. He maintains that until after the Napoleonic Invasion Spain was united by a religious fervor whose instrument was the Holy

Office. However, after the Peninsular War an attempt was made to supplant this with patriotism and the inspiration of the armed forces. Such an endeavor was vain, resulting in the regional divisions and the internecine warfare from which the Spanish nation had suffered in the nineteenth century.

This is the only point in the course of the three novels in which Valle-Inclán gives direct expression to his own opinion that the military had a detrimental effect on modern Spanish history. For the rest it is left to the reader to determine whether Valle remains a die-hard Carlist[16] or has undergone a radical change of political ideology. In my opinion some of the statements in these novels are irreconcilable. Narváez, on his deathbed, appears to be speaking with the author's own voice when he says that what Spain needs is "Carlism without clerical frocks,"[17] and in the same novel a humble Carlist who shares a railway compartment with Bonifaz and Torre Mellada is given very sympathetic treatment. On the other hand, in *Military Tricks* it is made abundantly clear that the author's sympathies lie with the Anarchists and with the self-effacing Salvochea in particular. Consequently, it is my own belief that as Valle-Inclán's approach to politics was more emotional than rational, he harbored sympathies for both the extremes of the political spectrum, showing his usual impatience for the "bourgeois" in the center. This, of course, takes us back to his evident affection for the Galician gentry and the beggars in contrast with his scorn shown for the new middle class.

There is a remark in *The Crusaders of the Cause* which is pertinent to Valle's social appraisal of Spain in 1868. It is made by a tinker who comments that since Spain is led by ruffians and villains, it is only just that everyone be allowed to behave after the same fashion.[18] This is precisely the philosophy carried into effect by the citizens of the *Iberian Ring*. What Valle reveals is that the corruption in the higher echelons of society has spread to the very humblest Spanish citizens. The bandits are protected by the large landowners; an officer of the law will beat up an innocent man because of the tempting prospect of promotion; a group of young bloods throw a policeman out of a window as a joke; a man cares more about a mare with a ticklish throat than about a dying woman. There is a fundamental disregard for human life which has very disturbing undertones. It suggests a society which has completely lost its standard of values and is about to be plunged into chaos. This sense of disquiet is underscored by the episodes of violence punctuating these novels: the devastating flood in the fourth book of *The Court of Miracles* and the affray at the Solana Fair in *Hurrah for My Owner*.

The most interesting single feature of *Military Tricks* is that it sheds considerable light on Valle's indifference to the individual. In an early draft of the novel, *Una castiza de Samaria (A Castilian from Samaria)*, Michael Bakunin is not the Anarchist portrayed; instead, his place is filled by the Anarchist prince, Peter Kropotkin. The riveting feature about the switch of character is that Valle made none but the most essential changes—from "The Prince" to "The Master"—when he replaced one Anarchist by another. Otherwise the description of the two characters is the same:

> Prince Peter Kropotkin lit up his new quarters with the broad, be-whiskered smile of a Slav apostle. His clear eyes, as jovial as a peasant's, betrayed no amazement and his expression might be of living trust in man's charity. (*Una castiza de Samaria, La novela de hoy,* 10)
> The Master lit up his new quarters with the broad, bewhiskered smile of a Slav apostle. His clear eyes, as jovial as a peasant's, betrayed no amazement, and his expression might be of living trust in man's charity. (*Baza de espadas* AHR, 102)

Although satire aimed at the mawkish sentimentality of the popular literature of the period is a feature of all these novels, it is most pronounced in *Military Tricks*. Here the steerage passengers are all agog about a ruffian called Indalecio who is clapped in irons. They think he attacked Fermín Salvochea because of an outburst of jealousy, whereas, in fact, Inda made an attempt on the Anarchist's life to rob him. Inda plays to the gallery, pretending that it was indeed a crime of passion which he tried to perpetrate.

Something not yet mentioned is the artistic aspects of these novels. Like *The Tyrant* they are quite dramatic in form, consisting of short "scenes" in dialogue which are introduced and rounded off by brief descriptive passages. The animal analogies find their most original expression in these works, for the *Iberian Ring* is peopled by a bizarre fauna in which hands are visualized as seals' flippers and a girl's walk as a zebra's trot.

To make the distortion "mathematical," objects and animals are humanized. In *Military Tricks* a parrot ruffles its feathers so as to read a conspiratorial message sent to Admiral Topete; in the same novel an oil lamp ejects puffs of smoke, bored by the deliberations of the revolutionaries round the table. In *Hurrah for My Owner,* the dog belonging to a blind man is compared to Diogenes because of the patient way in which it endures the arrant nonsense talked at the table above it. Finally, the moon, in various guises, shows curiosity in the freakish world it illuminates. As common as animal analogies are those equating characters with actors. This is particularly marked in the case of the Torre Melladas. Carolina, who affects French mannerisms popular at this time with the Spanish aristocracy, is often seen as a languid actress of the Comédie Française.

It remains finally to assess the development of Valle-Inclán's novelistic technique from the *modernista* novels to those of the *esperpento* period. In many ways there is little change. Nearly all of Valle-Inclán's novels have a dramatic bias, and in all cases the author raises an artistic barrier which may be idealized *(modernismo)* or degraded *(esperpento)* between himself and the reader, preferring the indirect approach and believing that the characters should speak for themselves. However, novels such as those of the Carlist War trilogy are concerned with active Traditionalist propaganda, while in the *Iberian Ring* novels Valle is in a destructive, negative mood. Circumstances have turned him into an angry old man whose personal disillusionment with the state of his country is given concrete expression in his later novels. Something else which changes with the emergence of the *esperpento*—and this is as obvious in the novels as in the plays of the period—is the artistic stimulus; the jerky, telegraphic prose style of *The Tyrant* and the *Iberian Ring* cycle, coupled with their profusion of startling and complex images are much more modern than those of, say, *Saintly Flower* or the *Sonatas.*

CHAPTER 9

Valle-Inclán's Significance as a Writer

FROM much that has been said in the course of this study about the works of Valle-Inclán, it will have emerged that he was not a writer who either sought or was likely to appeal to a wide section of the reading public. Nor was he one on whom young writers might choose to model themselves, partly because his style, particularly in his later works, is virtually inimitable. Owing to the intricacies of both his esthetic and his style, Valle is an author who demands something more than the reader's passive attention. He may not have expected his public to devote a lifetime to the study of any one of his works— as Joyce is said to have remarked about *Finnegans Wake*—yet, if the complexities of his output are to be appreciated and his works savored to the full, it is necessary also to be familiar with the somewhat uncommon ideas on which they are based. For these reasons Valle-Inclán, like other Spanish novelists of the 1920's such as Pérez de Ayala or Gabriel Miró, is more likely to appeal to a minority willing to meet the author halfway by patient study of his work.

Some years ago Valle, together with the other novelists to whom I have just referred, was reproached by a Spanish author of the post-war generation for making such demands on his reading public. In a series of articles published in 1959,[1] the Catalan novelist Juan Goytisolo roundly condemned Valle-Inclán, Míro, Ayala and Benjamín Jarnés for failing to appeal to a wide reading public. Goytisolo feels strongly that these novelists forgot their responsibility to their readers, being guilty of indifference to the socio-political problems of their day. Without doubt this is a gross distortion of the facts: Valle-Inclán and his contemporaries may have concerned themselves but little with day-to-day events in the arena of Spanish politics, but were nonetheless deeply preoccupied with fundamental questions about Spanish character and history. Witness the concern shown by both Pérez de Ayala[2] and Valle-Inclán in the outdated concept of honor and the intransigent views of the Spaniard on adultery. Nor should one forget Miró's sensitive appraisal of Spanish provincial society in the Oleza novels with its condemnation of the unhealthy emphasis laid by the clergy on chastity and the martyrdom of saints and virgins. Like García Lorca in his *Gypsy Ballads*,[3] Miró shows how the psychological development of the young can be affected by this distorted representation of sex, leading in later years to sexual perversions and inversions.

It must be added, however, that the remarks I have made about Valle-Inclán's representing a minority art are ceasing to apply where his drama is concerned. Many of his plays, and in particular the trilogy *The Vandals*, were ignored for decades because when he wrote them Valle-Inclán was well ahead of his time in terms of stagecraft. As I have indicated elsewhere,[4] nothing could be further removed from the concept of the "well-made play" than this trilogy. But now that there is a more tolerant attitude in theatrical circles towards episodic and fragmentary works, there is a revival of interest in Valle's dramas. This is evident from the production of *Divine Words* in Paris (1963) and of *The Eagle Scutcheon* in Madrid (1966).

The later plays too were generally shrugged aside until quite recently. One reason for this may be their modernity in the context of the period in which they were written: it took public taste some time to catch up with Valle's *esperpentos*. Significantly, more than one critic has drawn a parallel between Valle-Inclán's later drama and the plays of Samuel Beckett and Ionesco. A fair example of this kind of comparison which, in my opinion, is quite valid is found in this extract from a review of a production of *Los cuernos de don Friolera:*

Post-war dramatists cannot comment on our tragic situation in tragic terms; therefore they create tragi-comedies because they are aware of man's pathetic weakness. Ionesco's or Beckett's characters wait but without faith, disillusioned and unable to suppress their anguish. In the same way the *esperpentos* reveal the hero's laughable inadequacies by fixing them in a concave distorting mirror.[5]

Such a comparison is valid in general terms only and would not stand up to detailed examination. But it is a fact that the overall picture, the disparaging attitude towards the human animal, the spirit of grimness, extreme pessimism and anguish, is similar in Valle's works of the 1920's to that of the two dramatists writing after the second world war.

Although Valle-Inclán's work was not conducive to happy imitations, he did provide a certain stimulus for García Lorca, as the latter's brother, Francisco, has noted.[6] Without a doubt the "popular" elements in Lorca's earlier dramatic pieces such as *The Loves of Don Perlimpín with Belisa in her Garden* or *The Prodigious Shoemaker's Wife* spring in the main from his knowledge of traditional puppet plays and other entertainments— such as blind men's ballads—which were enjoyed by the populace in earlier times. But it is also possible that Valle's *esperpento, Don Friolera's Horns,* with its use of puppets and the cuckolding of the protagonist, may have played its part in influencing Lorca's choice of themes and their presentation. Other elements these two writers have in common are their use of the Civil Guard to suggest evil or some menace to man's happiness, and the emphasis laid by both on the horse: by Valle-Inclán in *The Vandals* and by Lorca in his rural tragedies. Furthermore, as Francisco Lorca indicates, there exists in the works of both dramatists the same oscillation between farce and tragedy although Lorca, unlike Valle, resorts only occasionally to the grotesque.

Critics have often referred to a supposed link between the powerful novel *El señor presidente (Mr. President)* by the Guatemalan Miguel Angel Asturías and Valle-Inclán's *The Tyrant.*[6] In my opinion, whatever stimulus Asturias may have derived from the Spanish novelist is limited. Such similarities as do exist are superficial: both are about a macabre and oppressive Latin-American dictatorship and its effect on the populace; both are highly stylized, revealing an awareness of contemporary art movements. Finally, in both novels the authors give artistic form to the evil in the world they are depicting by resorting frequently to the grotesque. However, the differences in my opinion outweigh the similarities; for this reason it would appear preferable to speak in terms of a possible comparison rather than of a direct debt on Asturias' part. In the first place, the Guatemalan novelist had no need of any outside stimulus for he himself had first-hand experience of the monstrous dictatorship described in his novel. It follows that Valle's detachment is neither possible nor, indeed, sought by Asturias. According to the esthetic he had evolved by the time he wrote *The Tyrant,* Valle-Inclán alienates the reader's emotions. He is concerned not only with an indictment of a ruthless military dictatorship, but also with satire of the foreigners who exploit a backward country for their own venal ends; with esoteric cults as is evident from the structure of the novel and, finally, with a criticism of debased popular literature. Asturias, on the other hand, is too impassioned, too involved in his material to make such niceties possible. What he and others have experienced at the hands of the corrupt and ruthless Estrada Cabrera and the intense suffering and bitterness resulting from it, impart to the novel a subjective note not to be found in *The Tyrant*. In *Mr. President* there is a constant appeal to the reader's emotions which is absent in Valle-Inclán's novel. Finally *The Tyrant* ends with the overthrow of the evil Santos Banderas; the last chapter of *Mr. President* describes the symbolic degradation of an erstwhile favorite of the dictator. He is punished for his disloyalty by being condemned to eke out the remaining years of his life at the bottom of the dark pit which is his cell, tortured in spirit by exquisite refinements of pain in which the dictator is exceptionally well versed.

Before concluding, I should like to remark briefly on certain similarities between the later works of Valle-Inclán and the fiction of Camilo José Cela. Both writers show an interest in primitive mentalities and play on fundamental emotions such as fear, lust and rage. They share a grim outlook on the world which is expressed by having recourse to the grotesque, to satire, and to caricature. Valle's endeavor to appear detached from the circumstances and characters he describes is echoed by Cela, who signals out the importance of objectivity on the author's part in the prologues to both *Viaje a la Alcarria (Journey to Alcarria)* and *La colmena (The Hive)*. It is not my intention to suggest that Cela has undeniably been "influenced" by Valle-Inclán; the similarities I have mentioned may be purely fortuitous or, alternatively, may stem in part from their common Celtic background.

Thus, while Valle-Inclán is generally acknowledged to be a

writer of outstanding merit in Spain, he has nevertheless not attracted a great deal of attention beyond a limited circle of admirers; readers who have become aware after an examination of his works that these offer more than mere verbal pyrotechnics.[7] In terms of his scant impact on a wider audience, he is a true inheritor of Symbolism, for what may be said of him applies also to James Joyce and the later poetry of Juan Ramón Jiménez. They are artists who to a greater or lesser degree have paid the cost of their own idiosyncratic erudition.

Notes and References

Chapter One

Author's note: All quotations from the works of Valle-Inclán, except where otherwise indicated, refer to the *Obras completas* (O.C.) in two volumes published by Plenitud (Madrid, 1954).

1. The author was in time to change his name from Valle Peña to del Valle-Inclán. No doubt this was done because he preferred its greater euphony and aristocratic ring.

2. See article by E. Correa Calderón, "La terrible infancia," *Revista de Occidente*, nos. 44-45 (Nov.-Dec., 1966), 330-41.

3. See Rosa Seeleman, "Folkloric elements in Valle-Inclán," *Hispanic Review*, III (1935), 103-18, and Rita Posse, "Notas sobre el folklore gallego en Valle-Inclán," *Cuadernos Hispanoamericanos*, nos. 44-5 (July-Aug., 1966), 493-520.

4. There is, for example, the contrast drawn between the aristocracy and the upstart bourgeoisie in the short story "Le dessous de cartes d'une partie de whist" from the collection *Les diaboliques* with which Valle was familiar from an early age.

5. See my article "Dandy elements in the Marqués de Bradomín *Hispanic Review*, XXXII (1964), 340-50.

6. The position and ideals of the Carlists in nineteenth-century Spain bear a certain resemblance to those of the Jacobites in Scotland a century before.

7. See Pedro Laín Entralgo, *La generación del noventa y ocho* (Buenos Aires: Espasa Calpe, 1947) and Hans Jeschke, *La generación del noventa y ocho* (Madrid: Nacional, 1945).

8. It is also interesting to note, with the irony provided by hindsight, that the writer who was to acquire renown above all as a stylist, failed an examination in Castilian language!

9. Many of these articles and short stories have been collected and published by Professor William Fichter in his work *Valle-Inclán's Newspaper Contributions before 1895 (Publicaciones periodísticas de Valle-Inclán anteriores a 1895)*. This volume was published in Mexico in 1952 by the Colegio de Méjico.

10. In *Sonata de verano,* however, the description is applied to the Bay of Grijalba, while in the earlier "The Mexican Princess" it is used to describe the coastal town of Progreso. This apparently arbitrary use of a set description applied to a number of places is, as I shall show later, but one example of Valle's scorn of the external differences to be observed in men and objects in the sensory world.

11. Luckily, from Valle's point of view, he was on close terms with a cultured resident of Pontevedra called Don Jesús de Muruais. In the latter's library the emphasis was on contemporary French works and, naturally enough, the aspiring author had free access to it.

·12. This experience, however, did not bring his career as an actor to an abrupt end. Shortly afterwards he took a small part in a play called *Les rois en exil* translated into Spanish by a fellow bohemian, Alejandro Sawa, whom Valle was to immortalize years later in the character of Max Estrella, the protagonist of *Bohemian Lights*. Much later in life Valle-Inclán took a number of parts in an impromptu, amateur production of Zorrilla's *Don Juan Tenorio* organized at the home of the Baroja brothers.

13. Valle later made certain changes in this play and altered its title to *El yermo de las almas (The Waste Lands of the Soul).*

14. Although this appears very strange in retrospect, the book is respectfully dedicated to the novelist Armando Palacio Valdés whose production, one would have thought, was totally alien to Valle-Inclán. For further details see D. Gamallo Fierros, "Aportaciones al estudio de Valle-Inclán," *Revista de Occidente,* nos. 44-45 (1966), 343-66.

15. Published in *La Revista Nueva* (Madrid).

16. For a brief definition of *Ultraísmo* see note 49 of chapter 2.

17. For a more detailed account of the events described, see Melchor Fernández Almagro, *Historia del reinado de Alfonso XIII* (Barcelona: Montaner y Simón, 1933).

18. Salvador de Madariaga, *Spain* (London: Jonathan Cape, 1942), 263.

19. J. B. Avalle Arce, "Las Españas de Valle-Inclán," *Spanish Thought and Letters in Twentieth-Century Spain* (Vanderbilt University Press: Nashville, 1966), pp. 51-62.

20. Valle-Inclán may well have borne in mind the example of Rubén Darío, whose work suffered owing to the poet's need to live by journalism.

21. In 1958, to be precise, by the Editorial AHR (Barcelona). Since then it has also appeared in the Austral Collection (Espasa Calpe: Buenos Aires, 1961).

Chapter Two

1. The reason for Valle-Inclán's indifference to originality, par-

ticularly in terms of character portrayal has a philosophical basis, and will be discussed in the next chapter.

2. There are evident exceptions: for example, his documentation of the ambitious cycle of historical novels, whose general title was *El ruedo ibérico (The Iberian Ring)*, is most impressive.

3. Fernández Almagro, "Teatro al margen," *Insula*, IX, no. 100-1 (1954), 7.

4. Enid Starkie, *Arthur Rimbaud* (London: Faber & Faber, 1938), 98.

5. See Jean Pommier, *La Mystique de Baudelaire* (Paris: Les Belles Lettres, 1932), pp. 16-17, 29.

6. The Symbolist poet, as A. G. Lehmann notes in his study *The Symbolist Aesthetic in France* (Oxford: Basil Blackwell, 1950), 47, ". . . was seeking an unrestricted range of expression, free from the formal and emotional patterns imposed by a realistic art; and turning from a philosophy whose avowed aim was a reasoned account of the exact determining forces in every sphere of knowledge and experience, . . . found for a time his haven in garbled versions of idealist epistemologies."

7. It is worth quoting a prose translation in full:
Nature is a temple where living pillars sometimes allow confused words to escape; man passes there through forests of symbols that watch him with familiar glances.
Like long drawn-out echoes mingled far away into a deep and shadowy unity, vast as darkness and light, scents, colours and sounds answer one another.
There are some scents cool as the flesh of children, sweet as oboes and green as meadows,—and others corrupt, rich and triumphant,
Having the expansion of things infinite, like amber, musk, benzoin and incense, singing the raptures of the mind and senses.
(*The Penguin Book of French Verse*, III [Penguin Books: Middlesex, 1957], 155.)

8. There is a passage in "L'Art romantique" in which Baudelaire dwells on Swedenborg's conception of the universe. See Guy Michaud, *La doctrine symboliste* (Paris: Nizet, 1947), 22.

9. See Pommier, chapter III: "L'Analogie universelle."

10. Quoted by Pommier, 74.

11. Starkie, *Rimbaud*, pp. 114-15.

12. In her study *From Gautier to Eliot* (London: Hutchinson, 1960), 89, Enid Starkie maintains that except for Villiers de L'Isle Adam, the Symbolists had no detailed knowledge of Wagner's music but used music in general as therapy, something like soaking in a warm, perfumed bath.

13. Wagner's most important contribution in terms of artistic theory is contained in his volume *Oper und Drama* (Leipzig, 1869).

14. This is the view of the American Symbolist Stuart Merrill as expressed in a letter to another poet of the movement, Vielé Griffin, in 1887. Quoted by Michaud, 74.

15. Edouard Schuré, *The Great Initiates* (London: William Rider, 1912), xxii-xxiii.

16. See Schuré, 85.

17. Quoted by Vincent Hopper, *Medieval Number Symbolism* (Columbia University Press, 1938), 33-34.

18. The number four represented Divinity because the addition of the first four numbers produces ten, the perfect number, representing as it does all the principles of divinity developed and reunited in a new unity. The first four numbers contain all the essential principles because all others are formed by adding or multiplying them.

19. See Starkie, 100. The Cabala (or Kabbala) was a Jewish esoteric philosophy concerned primarily with the mysteries of God, the Universe and all creation. The name is derived from the Hebrew term *Kabel* (to receive) and implies that special knowledge is accorded to the elect by way of revelation. The saintly few who received the esoteric doctrine transmitted it in turn to a select group capable of mastering the mystic lore. Cabala was also linked with many occult sciences such as astrology, alchemy and chiromancy.

20. Schuré, 39.

21. As Victor White indicates in his study *God and the Unconscious* (London: Harvill Press, 1952), 196, it is necessary to distinguish between Gnosis and a Gnostic. "The distinction," White maintains, "is of importance, if only because it is a profound mistake to suppose that, in rejecting gnosticism, the main body of the Christian Church thereby rejected gnosis or could find no room for the Gnostic. It neither did—nor could. The revelation which the Church herself accepted, and which gave her her very *raison d'être* was in itself in its origins a gnosis."

22. According to certain Gnostic myths the fallen eon is ultimately readmitted into the Pleroma owing to its redemption by Jesus.

23. White, *God and the Unconscious*, 197.

24. Quoted by Michaud, 15. The italics are my own.

25. See González Sobejano, "Epater le bourgeois en la España de 1900." *Wort und Text. Festschrift für Fritz Schalk* (Frankfurt am Main: Klostermann, 1963).

26. For example, Greek myths figure prominently in Rubén Darío's erotic poems. The reason for this is that lust appears less crude if decked out in glamorous apparel. It is in precisely this way that Darío uses the Jupiter-Leda myth.

27.   In this respect *Modernismo* resembles a later movement, namely *Ultraísmo*. Whereas the former is a compendium of literary theories current in the second half of the nineteenth century, the latter is a medley of certain ideas behind the avant-garde movements of the first two decades of the present century.

28.   F. L. Lucas, *The Decline and Fall of the Romantic Ideal* (Cambridge University Press, 1938), 120.

29.   *The Works of Oscar Wilde* (London: Collins, 1960), p. 909.

30.   Mention has already been made of the library in Pontevedra to which Valle had access and where the emphasis was on contemporary French literature.

31.   Juan Ramón Jiménez, "Ramón del Valle-Inclán: Castillo de quema," *El Sol* (Madrid), 26 January, 1936.

32.   Valle mentions that before choosing the way of the mystic he dabbled in the occult. This is because magic is traditionally used as a shortcut by those intent on releasing themselves from the bonds of the flesh. It accounts also for Rimbaud's interest in these very things, for his objective was the same as Valle-Inclán's.

33.   *La lámpara*, II, 567-68.

34.   *Ibid.*, 564.

35.   "Dante's circles are the most tragic representation of futile pride . . . Satan, sterile and proud, longs to be present in the All. Satan whirls eternally in the Horus of the Pleroma." *Ibid.*, 566.

36.   "The instants of time opened out like the circles of long lives and due to their singular magnitude everything was revealed to my senses graced by a new meaning." *Ibid.*, 564.

37.   "With a deep and fulsome joy I felt myself bound to the mountain crag, the shadow of the tree and the flight of the bird." *Ibid.*, 562.

38.   See, for example, 560.

39.   Speaking of the poet as a wonder-worker, he writes: "In the Pythagorean numbers he encloses Platonic Ideas." *Ibid.*, 582.

40.   "Chronological knowledge became static and souls were divested of memory so as to learn along the divine way of the Sun." *Ibid.*, 581.

41.   See 591, 594.

42.   *Ibid.*, 570-71.

43.   *Ibid.*, 571.

44.   *Ibid.*, 577.

45.   *Loc cit.*

46.   *Le Chateau d'Axel* (Paris: Quantin, 1889), p. 283.

47.   Salinas, *Literatura española siglo veinte* (México: Robredo, 1948), pp. 87-114.

48. *Sonata de invierno* (Madrid: Revista de archivos, bibliotecas y museos, 1905) II, 228.

49. I have already alluded in passing to the *ultraísta* movement, but it is worth providing a few more details. Like the *modernistas,* against whom they were reacting, the *ultraístas* saw themselves as the pioneers of a literary renewal. It was their avowed intent to "synchronize their watches with Europe." To this end they borrowed freely from Cubists, Futurists and Expressionists, producing a rather uneasy compromise based on all these movements. *Ultraísmo* was shortlived, one reason for this being that it produced no single outstanding writer. However, some of those who subscribed to it in a moment of youthful enthusiasm were to acquire fame later in life. Among these are the highly original Argentine writer Jorge Luis Borges and the Spanish literary critic Guillermo de Torre.

50. The *Callejón del gato* or Cat's Walk was an alleyway famous in Madrid for the distorting mirrors that flanked it.

51. *Luces de bohemia,* I, 939.

52. See Gregorio Martínez Sierra, "Hablando con Valle-Inclán, de él y de su obra," *ABC* (Madrid), 7 December, 1928, 12.

Chapter Three

1. One example is the preposterous and blood-curdling fancies found in the autobiographical fragment published in *Alma Española* (December 27, 1903), which bear a marked similarity to certain incidents in the *Summer Sonata* published in the same year.

2. Manuel Durán, "La técnica de la novela y la generación del noventa y ocho," *Revista Hispánica Moderna,* XXIII (1957), 14-27.

3. José Ortega y Gasset, *La deshumanización del arte* (Madrid: Revista de Occidente), 1925, 33.

4. It should be pointed out that violence is not axiomatic in the plays of the interim period which have an atmosphere of sensual refinement and delicacy.

5. See, for example, such stories as "A medianoche," "Zan el de los osos" and "Un cabecilla."

6. As is often the case with titles devised by Valle-Inclán, it is virtually impossible to render this one adequately in translation. *Trueno* refers both to thunder and to a society formed in Madrid in the 1830's by wealthy youths. These delighted in defying authority and upsetting the more sober citizens of Madrid with their rather childish practical jokes. Larra describes their activities in his sketch of "el calavera temerón" which is found in the second of his two articles dedicated to "Los calaveras" ("The Roués").

7. Quoted by Pedro Laín Entralgo in *La generación del noventa y ocho* (Madrid: Diana, 1945), 206.

8. Quoted by A. Valbuena Prat in *Historia de la literatura española*, III (Barcelona: Gustavo Gilí, 1953), 512.

9. Fichter, *Publicaciones*, pp. 20-21.

10. Serenín de Bretal appears as a blind man in the short story "Mi bisabuelo." In the play *Divinas palabras* he is an elderly peasant toiling in the fields with his grandchildren. He makes a third appearance, cast once again as a peasant, in the short story "Milon de la Arnoya."

11. Thus a Duque de Ordax appears in the early short story "Rosita," in *Gerifaltes de antaño* and in *La corte de los milagros*. A further example that might be quoted is that of the notary Malvido who symbolizes the grasping upstarts of the new middle class. He figures in both *Aguila de blasón* and "Mi bisabuelo"; nor can it be doubted that if in the *Sonata de otoño* Don Juan Manuel Montenegro had cared to identify the notary he is about to beat, his name too would have been Ambrosio Malvido.

12. See note 7, p. 162 and note 12, p. 164.

13. See above, pp. 38-39.

14. "At Midnight" (1889). See Fichter, *Publicaciones*, 50.

15. "La cabeza del bautista," (1924). *O.C.*, I, 877.

16. *Viva mi dueño*, (1928). *O.C.*, II, 1193.

17. "Mi hermana Antonia" (1909). *O.C.*, I, 1273.

18. *Los cuernos de don Friolera* (1921). *O.C.*, I, 1031.

19. See above, 40.

20. See, for example, Salvador de Madariaga's observations in *The Genius of Spain and Other Essays* (Oxford: Clarendon Press, 1923), 146.

21. In the *Nueva Revista de Filología Hispánica*, VII (1953), 526-35.

22. See above, 20.

23. *Revista Hispánica Moderna*, XXV (1959), 57-80.

24. These were in chronological order "Sonata de otoño," "Don Juan Manuel," "Hierba santa," "Corazón de niña," "El palacio de Brandeso" and, lastly, "El miedo."

25. In "Rosita" the heroine is in fact the Queen of Dalicam as she is married to the Indian monarch of this kingdom. Consequently there can be little doubt that "Rosita" is but a reelaboration of the earlier short story which I have been unable to see.

26. Notebooks and correspondence are in the possession of Valle-Inclán's son Carlos who kindly allowed me to see them.

27. *O.C.*, II, 632.

28. See E. S. Speratti Piñero, *La elaboración artística en "Tirano Banderas"* (Mexico: El Colegio de Mexico, 1957). A resumé of the plot of *Tirano Banderas* is given on pp. 128-30 of this study.

29. Díaz-Plaja, *Las estéticas* . . . (Madrid: Gredos, 1965), 99.

30. Franco, "The Concept of Time in *El ruedo ibérico*," *Bulletin of Hispanic Studies*, XXXIX (1962), 177-87.

31. See Hopper, *Number Symbolism*, 43.

32. I am indebted to Professor Gerard Cox Flynn for indicating this point to me.

33. In evolving his theory of the eternal recurrence of all events, Nietzsche, like Schopenhauer before him, had recourse to Oriental philosophy. Thus it is possible that Nietzsche's doctrine served to confirm the importance of Eastern thought in Valle's eyes.

34. The author's son, Dr. Carlos del Valle-Inclán, kindly allowed me to make a copy of this letter which remains unpublished.

35. See A. A. Mendilow, *Time and the Novel* (London & New York: Peter Nevill, 1952) and Joseph Frank, "Spatial Form in Modern Literature," *The Sewanee Review* (1945), 230-40.

36. Ortega y Gasset, *Ideas sobre la novela* (Madrid: Revista de Occidente, 1925).

37. *Op. cit.*, 92.

38. Joyce, *Portrait of the Artist as a Young Man* (London: The Egoist, 1916), 252.

39. An example of the use of this technique is to be found in *Tirano Banderas* when the author describes the disconnected thoughts surging through the mind of one of the characters (Barón Benicarlés) after he has given himself a shot of morphine.

40. In an interview Valle-Inclán spoke of his purpose in *El ruedo ibérico* in the following terms: ". . . what I am aiming at, rather than a novel of action, is satire disguised by conventions which are almost those of the theater. I say almost of the theater because everything is expressed through dialogues and my opinions are not expressed directly." See Gregorio Martínez Sierra, *ABC* (1936), 9-10.

41. This art of juxtaposition or *montage* is described by Roger Shattuck (*The Banquet Years* [London: Faber & Faber, 1959], 256) in the following way:
"Had the montage form of art been concerned with a real succession of events, transition would have been included rather than suppressed, for transition provides an order of events. Ultimately it becomes apparent that mutually conflicting elements of montage—be it film, poem or painting—are to be conceived not successively but simultaneously, to converge in our minds as contemporaneous events. The conflict between them prevents us from fitting them smoothly end to end; what appears an arbitrary juxtaposition of parts can now take its shape of imposed superposition . . . The aspiration of simultanism is to grasp the moment in its total significance, or, more ambitiously, to manufacture a moment which surpasses our usual perception of time and space."

Chapter Four

1. Gerardo Diego, *Poesía española* (Madrid: Taurus, 1959), 85.

2. See in particular "Los pobres de Dios," *O.C.*, I, 1082-83.

3. Written in Galician-Portuguese by King Alfonso X of Castile (1221-1284).

4. *O.C.*, I, 1094.

5. *Ibid.*, 1093.

6. *Ibid.*, 1134, 1137.

7. *Ibid.*, 419.

8. Ortega, *Deshumanización*, 24.

9. Valle-Inclán alludes to both Goya and Solana in "El crimen de Medinica," *O.C.*, I, 1161-63.

10. *Ibid.*, 1162.

11. *Ibid.*, 1140.

12. *Ibid.*, 1149.

13. See in particular "Rosa de bronce" (*ibid.*, 1121-22) and "Rosa de pecado" (1117-18).

14. "Rosa del caminate," *ibid.*, 1101-2.

15. *Ibid.*, 1124.

16. This allegory is used by Plato in *The Republic* to contrast the world of phenomena with that of Ideas or Forms. Adapting the allegory for a modern audience—as H.D.P. Lee suggests in his translation (Penguin Classics, 1955)—Plato's illustration is as follows: The human race, in contemporary terms, is seen as a motion picture audience and what they consider to be "reality" is but an image projected onto a screen. Occasionally a solitary individual, by dint of untiring effort, is able to leave the darkened hall and to stagger forth into the light of day and the true world. Thus the flat images on the screen are to be equated with the world of the senses and the sunlit zone outside the building with the superior and unchanging world of Forms.

17. *O.C.*, I, 1118-19.

18. *Ibid.*, 1108.

Chapter Five

1. Alonso Zamora Vicente, *Las Sonatas de Valle-Inclán* (Madrid: Gredos, 1955), 133.

2. See above, Chap. I.

3. See Melchor Fernández Almagro, *Vida y literatura de Valle-Inclán* (Madrid: Nacional, 1943), 167.

4. Similar characteristics are to be found in "La confesión" (1892) and "Eulalia" from the collection *Corte de amor* (1903).

5. Juan Guerrero Zamora, *Historia del teatro contemporáneo*, I (Barcelona: Juan Flors, 1961), 169.

6.   *Aguila de blasón,* the most rambling of the *Comedias bárbaras,* was produced in Madrid early in 1966.

7.   In his study of Valle-Inclán, to which I have already referred, Díaz-Plaja develops an interesting theory on the three Don Juan figures in Valle's works. In this critic's opinion each one is a recognizable symbol of a particular phase in the author's work. See *Las estéticas de Valle-Inclán,* pp. 141-51.

8.   Valle wrote three novels about the Carlist War and conceived of the *Ruedo ibérico* cycle in three series, each series to consist of three novels.

9.   *O.C.,* I, 500.

10.   *Ibid.,* 547-48.

11.   *Ibid.,* 556.

12.   The use of this figure is a further example of Valle-Inclán's proclivity for characters with an established literary background. Millers' wives are traditionally lascivious and of easy virtue. Chaucer draws on precisely the same tradition in *The Reeve's Tale.* The same applies to Valle-Inclán's sacristans for, again, there is an established literary convention whereby sacristans are deceitful and weak. This convention is always adhered to by Valle-Inclán.

13.   It should be noted that Valle-Inclán's stage directions are not intended merely to help a producer. They are exquisite prose passages which add to the artistic value of the work.

14.   Franco Meregalli, *Studi su Valle-Inclán* (Venice: Libreria Universitaria, 1958), 28.

15.   *O.C.,* I, 721.

16.   Three of the farces were later collected in a single volume and published under the general heading of *A Marionette Theater for the Benefit of Princes (Tablado de marionetas para educación de príncipes),* 1926. They were *Farsa y licencia de la reina castiza (Farce of the Castilian Queen), La cabeza del dragón (The Dragon's Head),* and *Farsa de la enamorada del rey (Farce of the Maid Who Loved a King).*

17.   There is one very witty jibe directed at a pseudo-scholar who is about to be given a Chair in the Academy of Literature. He is responsible for determining how many times the word "inn" appears in *Don Quixote.*

18.   The action takes place in a Castilian roadside inn. Describing it in the initial stage direction, Valle notes that the building carries "a whiff of Don Quixote's prose." (*O.C.,* I, 316)

19.   It is possible that both the Prologue given by Harlequin and the notion of including other *commedia dell'arte* characters are due to the appearance in 1909 of Jacinto Benavente's play *Los intereses creados.*

20.   *O.C.,* I, 230.

21. *Ibid.*, 301.

22. *Ibid.*, 435.

23. In *Farsa de la cabeza del dragón* there is a delightful vignette of a fire-eating general called Fierabrás. It emerges that he has been awarded all his medals for combatting drunkenness and that he received his nickname—implying he is bold and fierce—from his wife because of his uncertain temper when about the house.

24. *O.C.*, I, 463.

25. The King Consort is visualized as an ostrich hiding his head under a wing; the Lord Chamberlain rushes away with the vertiginous speed of a cat, and elderly court ladies busy gossiping are seen as birds with prominent beaks.

26. *O.C.*, I, 440.

Chapter Six

1. Valle-Inclán's son, Carlos, showed me another *esperpento* which remains unpublished because of its scant literary merit.

2. It is virtually impossible to do justice to this title in translation as it involves a play on words. *Martes de carnaval* can indeed be translated simply as *Shrove Tuesday*, but *Martes* also evokes Mars, god of war, in the plural form. Thus the title also implies warriors who are figures of fun. Furthermore, Shrove Tuesday is followed immediately by Ash Wednesday so that, by implication, Valle is hinting that disaster is imminent. Another title which defies adequate translation is *La corte de los milagros (The Court of Miracles)*. The French expression *cour des miracles* was used in Paris in medieval times to describe a thieves' kitchen.

3. See in particular J. L. Brooks, "Valle-Inclán and the *esperpento*," *Bulletin of Hispanic Studies*, XXXIII (1956), 152-64. According to this critic there is only one *esperpento* that meets all the requirements of the genre, this being *Don Friolera's Horns*. I disagree with this contention because the finest *esperpento* is taken as a yardstick for the others. The fact that they do not fully measure up to it is not a valid reason to exclude them from the genre.

4. For some unknown reason Valle also chose to include the much earlier play *El embrujado (A Man Bewitched)*, 1913, in this collection. Its tone is completely out of keeping with that of the later playlets.

5. In her study of the German Expressionist film *L'Ecran démoniaque* (Paris: Cahiers du Cinema, 1952), Lotte Eisner (p. 140) describes the aims of the Expressionist as follows: "The Expressionist artist endeavors to record not a fleeting sensation but the eternal significance of things. According to the Expressionists one must seek

to detach oneself from nature and try to wrest the most meaningful expression from an object."

6.   *O.C.*, I, 914.

7.   See Anthony Zahareas, "The *esperpento* and esthetics of commitment," *Modern Language Notes* (March, 1966), 159-73. Zahareas does not dwell on one essential point, namely that *Bohemian Lights* shows Valle's complete indifference to chronology. For in 1920 Bradomín would have been almost 110 years old (see note 12, p. 164) and the poet Rubén Darío died in 1916.

8.   When Valle seeks to pour scorn on some high-ranking official he often does so by making him appear ridiculous, that is, by describing him in a state of disarray or partial undress. This is one of his devices in the later works, applying not only to the minister, don Paco, in this play, but also to Friolera's superior, Colonel Pancho Lamela, to Brigadier Topete in *Military Tricks* and also to the military commander, El marqués de los Llanos, in the short work *Fin de un revolucionario (End of a Revolutionary)*.

9.   As Valle-Inclán explains when defining the *esperpento*, the genre involves "mathematical distortion," that is, a complete reversal of the accepted social order. A further example of mathematical distortion is that a patriotic slogan such as "Long Live Spain" is uttered by a parrot. (*O.C.*, I, 896)

10.   *O.C.*, I, 933.

11.   Like the high-ranking official found at his toilet or scantily attired, the dead child is a set piece or emblem in Valle's works. It suggests, obviously enough, that it is the innocent who suffer. Other instances are to be found in *Spring Sonata, A Man Bewitched, Divine Words, Don Friolera's Horns,* and *The Tyrant*.

12.   *O.C.*, I, 938.

13.   *Ibid.*, 951-52.

14.   Espronceda's original line is "What is one more corpse to the world?"

15.   *O.C.*, I, 899.

16.   E. S. Speratti Piñero, *La elaboración artística en Tirano Banderas* (Mexico: Fondo de Cultura Económica, 1957), pp. 103-4.

17.   The anti-hero, Juanti Ventolera, says at one point: "All they are doing there [Cuba] is to waste munitions. If the soldier knew where his duty lay and weren't a serf he would fire on his commanding officers." (*O.C.*, I, 965)

18.   See J. B. Avalle-Arce, "La esperpentización de Don Juan," *Hispanófila*, III (1959), 29-39.

19.   *O.C.*, I, 993.

20.   *Ibid.*, 995.

21.   *Ibid.*, 996.

22. *Ibid.*, 999.
23. *Ibid.*, 102.
24. *Ibid.*, 1045.
25. *Ibid.*, 1010.
26. *Ibid.*, II, 258.
27. According to Lavater the external appearance of a person corresponds to his spiritual make-up. Furthermore, "every individual is a harmony," that is, it is possible to determine the appearance of the whole from a particular part of the body. Thus Lavater praises Goya for having created "harmonious" monsters. This is of interest in that Valle-Inclán also admired Goya for the "mathematical distortion" of the figures. On Lavater, see Pommier, *Mystique*, 52.
28. The reference to a cat and a frog are not fortuitous. In the *esperpento* period Valle-Inclán became deeply interested in Goya and there are two sketches for the *Caprichos* and *Esperpentos* which are of relevance in this context. One of them shows an army officer staring into a mirror: the reflection shows a cat with bristling whiskers and reproachful gaze. In another a woman is faced with a serpent coiled round the haft of Time's scythe. She is accompanied by a male figure contemplating in astonishment a frog.
29. See for example, *O.C.*, I, 1005, 1006, 1007, 1030.
30. *Ibid.*, 1027.
31. *Ibid.*, 1040.
32. See Díaz-Plaja, *Estéticas*, pp. 143-4.
33. *O.C.*, I, 890. The events described in this play have been discreetly lifted from the finest novel of the Mexican writer Mariano Azuela. I refer, of course, to *Los de abajo* (1915).
34. It is apparent from his very earliest literary exercises that Valle brought a painter's eye to writing. He was fascinated, above all, by the effects achieved with light and shade and colored shadows.
35. *O.C.*, I, 815.
36. *Ibid.*, 822.
37. *Ibid.*, 820.
38. Gino Nenzioni, "Gli 'esperpentos' (a proposito del teatro di Ramón del Valle-Inclán)," *Letteratura Moderne*, IX (1959), 73.

Chapter Seven

1. "Augusta" had been published in 1897 under the title of "Epitalamio."
2. Like "Augusta," "Beatriz" had been published before under a different title, "Satanás" (1901). Valle entered this short story in a contest sponsored by the newspaper *El Liberal* but did not receive an award since the contents were considered too macabre and horrific by the judges.

3. Díaz-Plaja, *Estéticas,* pp. 201-13. The three Don Juan figures in question are the ironic (Bradomín), the heroic (don Juan Manuel Montenegro), and the debased (Juanito Ventolera in the *esperpento The Dead Man's Finery).*

4. Salinas, *Literatura siglo XX,* 16.

5. See José Alberich, "Ambigüedad y humorismo en las *Sonatas* de Valle-Inclán," *Hispanic Review,* XXXIII (1965), 360-82.

6. The incident involving a witch is a direct borrowing from Casanova's *Memoirs.*

7. *O.C.,* II, 62.

8. *Ibid.,* 87.

9. The homosexual Russian and his father make a brief reappearance in *Winter Sonata.* This, together with an allusion in the same novel to *Spring,* is the sum of Valle's attempts—apart from the Marquis himself—to give the *Sonatas* some measure of unity.

10. *O.C.,* II, 82.

11. *Ibid.,* 63.

12. The allusion to their childhood games is an example of Valle's indifference to chronological time. *Autumn Sonata* takes place around the year 1870. (Concha refers to the Pretender's wife Margarita and to "the other one" who in the context must be Isabel II. In addition she says of "the other one" that she was always much maligned, which suggests that Isabel has already been deposed [1868]). At this juncture Concha is thirty-one. But Bradomín was twenty in *Spring* which is set in the early 1830's; he must therefore be close to sixty when he stays with Concha at Brandeso. Consequently chronology is treated here in the same cavalier fashion as in *Bohemian Lights.*

13. Zamora Vicente, 142.

14. Enrique Anderson Imbert, "El escamoteo de la realidad en las *Sonatas* de Valle-Inclán," *Realidad* (Buenos Aires), II (1948), 47.

15. *O.C.,* I, 1178.

16. Rosa Seeleman, "Folkloric elements in Valle-Inclán," *Hispanic Review,* III (1935), 115.

17. *O.C.,* I, 1225.

18. *Ibid.,* 1227.

19. This letter is in the possession of Valle-Inclán's son Carlos.

20. Valle-Inclán's journey to Navarre is described by his son in the prologue to *Gerfalcons of Yore* (Buenos Aires: Austral, 1945).

21. The author indicates indirectly that much of the fault is Bradomín's. The Marquis is too proud to deal personally with someone of Ginero's type, and is conscious that by delegating responsibility to his steward he is bound to be fleeced.

22. *O.C.,* II, 383.

23. *Ibid.,* 383.

24. *Ibid.*, 381.
25. *Ibid.*, 363.
26. *The Crusaders of the Cause* takes place only a very short time after *Autumn Sonata*. It will be recalled that in the latter novel Isabel de Bendaña is a young woman who has taken no religious vows. Now she is transformed into the elderly Mother Superior of a convent. Yet the author makes it quite clear that this is the same person because he mentions that Bradomín and Concha are her cousins (*O.C.*, II, 351). It is unlikely that this is a careless oversight but, instead, a further example of Valle's conscious refutation of individuality and chronological time.
27. *O.C.*, II, 380.
28. *Ibid.*, 353.
29. *Ibid.*, 448.
30. Others in the long gallery of warrior priests are Fray Ambrosio in *Winter Sonata;* Don Benicio, the chaplain in "Rosarito"; the parish priest of San Rosendo de Gondar in the early short story "El rey de la máscara" ("The Carnival King"), 1892; the wicked Fray Angel in "Beatriz" and Doña María's chaplain in *The Eagle Scutcheon*.
31. *O.C.*, II, 505.
32. See above, 63.

Chapter Eight

1. "Autocrítica," *España*, 8 March, 1924, 150.
2. Gregorio Martínez Sierra, *ABC*, 7 December, 1928, 11.
3. *O.C.*, II, 780.
4. See Speratti Piñero, *Elaboración artística*, pp. 12-30.
5. *O.C.*, II, 830.
6. *Ibid.*, 705, 787.
7. *Ibid.*, 789.
8. *Ibid.*, 1065.
9. See C.A.M. Hennessy, *The Federal Republic in Spain* (Oxford: Clarendon Press, 1962), 3.
10. For a detailed analysis of the deliberate parallelisms and contrasts within each individual book of this and its sister novel *Hurrah for My Owner*, see H. L. Boudreau, "The circular structure of Valle-Inclán's *Ruedo ibérico*," *Publications of the Modern Language Association of America*, LXXXII (1967), 128-35.
11. *O.C.*, II, 985.
12. *Baza de espadas* (Buenos Aires: Austral, 1961), 176.
13. "Valle-Inclán," *ABC*, 8 January, 1936, 4.
14. See above pp. 123-4.
15. See Fernández Almagro, *Vida y literatura*, 252, and Franco Meregalli, *Studi su Valle-Inclán*, 52.

16. One critic who is convinced that Valle never lost his Carlist sympathies is Gaspar Gómez de la Serna. See his article "Las dos Españas de Valle-Inclán," *Clavileño*, III, no. 17 (1952), 17-32.

17. *O.C.*, II, 1024.

18. *Ibid.*, 369.

Chapter Nine

1. Juan Goytisolo, *Problemas de la novela* (Barcelona: Seix Barral, 1959). These articles first appeared in the weekly *Destino*.

2. This concern is much to the fore in Pérez de Ayala's novels *Tigre Juan* and its sequel *El curandero de su honra*. The title of the second novel parodies Calderón's drama *El médico de su honra*.

3. This question is considered in some detail by Arturo Barea in his study of Lorca entitled *Lorca: The Poet and his People* (London: Faber & Faber, 1944).

4. Above, 76.

5. Olga Brooks, 'Los cuernos de don Friolera en Londres,' *Insula*, no. 185 (1962), 15.

6. See Francisco García Lorca's introduction to Federico García Lorca's *Three Tragedies* (London: Penguin Books, 1961).

7. See, for example, Ricardo Navas Ruiz, *Literatura y compromiso* (Sao Paolo, 1962), and J. Liscano's "De Valle-Inclán a Miguel Angel Asturias," *Europe* (Paris), XXXVI (1958), 181-91.

8. Not that the pyrotechnics are to be scorned and, indeed, the very considerable difficulties facing the translator of Valle-Inclán account in part for his production not being better known outside of the Spanish-speaking world.

Selected Bibliography

PRIMARY SOURCES

1. *Femeninas* (Pontevedra: A. Landín, 1895).
2. *Epitalamio* (Madrid: Imprenta de Marzo, 1897).
3. *Cenizas* (Madrid: Bernardo Rodríguez y Perma, 1899).
4. *Sonata de otoño* (Madrid: A. Pérez, 1902).
5. *Jardín umbrío* (Madrid: Imprenta de la viuda de Rodríguez Sierra, 1903. Biblioteca Mignon, XXXVIII). An expanded version appeared in 1914.
6. *Corte de amor* (Madrid: A. Marzo, 1903).
7. *Sonata de estío* (Madrid: A. Marzo, 1903).
8. *Sonata de primavera* (Madrid: A. Marzo, 1904).
9. *Flor de santidad* (Madrid: A. Marzo, 1904).
10. *Sonata de invierno* (Madrid: Tipografía de la Revista de Archivos, Bibliotecas y Museos, 1905).
11. *Jardín novelesco* (Madrid: Tipografía de la Revista de Archivos, Bibliotecas y Museos, 1905). Second edition, with five short stories not found in the first (Barcelona: Maucci, 1908).
12. *Historias perversas* (Barcelona: Maucci, 1907).
13. *Aguila de blasón* (Barcelona: F. Granada, 1907).
14. *Aromas de leyenda* (Madrid: Villavicencio, Tipografía de la Revista de Archivos, Bibliotecas y Museos, 1907).
15. *El marqués de Bradomín* (Madrid: Tipografía de la Revista de Archivos, Bibliotecas y Museos, 1907).
16. *Romance de lobos* (Madrid: Pueyo, 1908).
17. *Los cruzados de las causa* (Madrid: Imprenta de Balgañon y Moreno, 1908).
18. *El yermo de las almas* (Madrid: Imprenta de Balgañon y Moreno, 1908).
19. *El resplandor de la hoguera* (Madrid: P. Fernandez, 1908-1909).
20. *Gerifaltes de antaño* (Madrid: P. Fernández, 1908-1909).
21. *Cofre de sándalo* (Madrid: P. Fernández, 1909). Contains four of the six short stories found in *Femeninas*.

22. *Cuento de abril* (Madrid: P. Fernández, 1910).

23. A fragment entitled "La corte de Estella" which the author may have intended to incorporate in the Carlist War trilogy was published in the periodical *Por esos mundos* in Jan., 1910.

24. *Las mieles del rosal* (Madrid: A. Marzo, 1910). Contains selections of Valle's prose works.

25. *Voces de gesta* (Madrid: Alemana, 1911).

26. *La marquesa Rosalinda* (Madrid: Alemana, 1913).

27. *El embrujado* (Madrid: J. Izquierdo, 1914).

28. *Farsa de la cabeza del dragón* (Madrid: J. Izquierdo, 1914).

29. *La lámpara maravillosa* (Madrid: Helénica, 1916).

30. *A medianoche* (Madrid: Clásica española, 1917).

31. *Mi hermana Antonia* (Madrid: José Blass, 1918).

32. *La pipa de kif* (Madrid: Clásica española, 1919).

33. *Cuentos, estética y poemas* (México: Tipografía Murguía, 1919).

34. *Farsa de la enamorada del rey* (Madrid: Gráfica Ambos Mundos, 1920).

35. *El pasajero* (Madrid: Yagües, 1920).

36. *Divinas palabras* (Madrid: Yagües, 1920).

37. *Farsa y licencia de la reina castiza* (Madrid: Artes de la Ilustración, 1922).

38. Dramatic interlude entitled "¿Para cuándo son las reclamaciones diplomáticas?" published in *España*, July 15, 1922.

39. *Cara de plata* (Madrid: Cervantina, 1923).

40. *Luces de bohemia* (Madrid: Cervantina, 1924).

41. *La rosa de papel* y *La cabeza del baustista* (Madrid: La Novela Semanal, March 22, 1924).

42. *Los cuernos de don Friolera* (Madrid: Cervantina, 1925).

43. *Tablado de marionetas para educación de príncipes* (Madrid: Rivadeneyra, 1926). Contains three farces which had already been published: *La cabeza del dragón*, *Farsa y licencia de la reina castiza* and *Farsa de la enamorada del rey*.

44. *Las galas del difunto* (Madrid: Sucesores de Rivadeneyra, 1926).

45. *Zacarías el cruzado* (Madrid: La Novela de Hoy, September 3, 1926).

46. *Tirano Banderas* (Madrid: Sucesores de Rivadeneyra, 1926).

47. *Retablo de la avaricia, la lujuria y la muerte* (Madrid: Rivadeneyra, 1927).

48. *La corte de los milagros* (Madrid: Rivadeneyra, 1927). The work was serialized in *El Sol* of Madrid, October-December, 1931. It starts with a new chapter, "Aires nacionales."

49. *La hija del capitán* (Madrid: La Novela Mundial, July 28, 1927).
50. *Teatrillo de enredo* (Madrid: Los Novelistas, June 28, 1928).
51. *Viva mi dueño* (Madrid: Rivadeneyra, 1928).
52. *Fin de un revolucionario* (Madrid: Prensa Moderna, 1928).
53. *Otra castiza de Samaria* (Madrid: La Novela de Hoy, November 15, 1929).
54. *Claves líricas* (Madrid: Rivadeneyra, 1930).
55. *Martes de carnaval* (Madrid: Rivadeneyra, 1930).
56. *Vísperas de La Gloriosa* (Madrid: La Novela de Hoy, May 16, 1930).
57. *El Sol* began publication in June 1932 of "Vísperas septembrinas," a section of the novel *Baza de espadas*. The complete novel appeared in 1958 (Barcelona: AHR).
58. In 1933 and 1935 the newspaper *Ahora* published a series of articles by Valle-Inclán on aspects of Spanish nineteenth-century history under the general title of *Correo diplomático*.
59. From March 19, 1936 to April 23, 1936, the newspaper *Ahora* published fragments of an unfinished novel, *El trueno dorado*, which was to have formed part of the *Ruedo ibérico* cycle.

SECONDARY SOURCES

ALAS, LEOPOLDO, (pseud. "Clarín"). "Palique," *Madrid Cómico*, 25 September, 1897. Witty, acid but not ungenerous evaluation of an example of Valle's juvenilia ("Epitalamio") by a critic who at the time could make or mar the reputation of an aspiring Spanish writer.

ALBERICH, J. "Ambigüedad y humorismo en las *Sonatas* de Valle-Inclán," *Hispanic Review*, XXXIII (1965), 360-82. Concerned with the humor implicit in the *Sonatas*.

ALONSO, AMADO. "Estructura de las *Sonatas* de Valle-Inclán," *Materia y Forma en Poesía* (Madrid: Gredos, 1955). Fundamental study of the *Sonatas* in which Alonso concentrates on three intertwined themes in these novels: eroticism, religion and death. Considers also Valle's possible debt to certain French nineteenth-century writers.

ANDERSON, IMBERT, E. "El escamoteo de la realidad en las *Sonatas* de Valle-Inclán," *Crítica interna* (Madrid: Taurus, 1961). Excellent article on author's esthetic in the *Sonatas*. Considers major themes such as religion and death.

AVALLE ARCE, J. B. "La esperpentización de Don Juan," *Hispanófila*, III (1959), 29-39. A definitive statement on Valle's *esperpento*, *The Dead Man's Finery*.

_____. "Las Españas de Valle-Inclán," *Spanish Thought and Letters in the Twentieth Century.* Ed. by G. Bleiberg and E. Inman Fox (Nashville: Vanderbilt University Press, 1966). Concludes that Valle felt sympathy for both extremes of the political spectrum.

BROOKS, J. L. "Valle-Inclán and the *esperpento,*" *Bulletin of Hispanic Studies,* XXXIII (1956), 152-64. An interesting but debatable interpretation of the *esperpento* genre.

_____. "Los dramas de Valle-Inclán," *Estudios dedicados a Menéndez Pidal,* VII (Madrid, 1957), 177-98. The twin streams, rural and urban, of Valle's theater: their development from the *Comedias bárbaras* to the *esperpentos* and the *Dramas of Avarice, Lust and Death.*

CASALDUERO, JOAQUIN. "Elementos funcionales en las *Sonatas* de Valle-Inclán," *Estudios de literatura española* (Madrid: Gredos, 1962). A penetrating article on the themes of eroticism, terror and sin in the *Sonatas.*

DIAZ-PLAJA, GUILLERMO. *Modernismo frente a noventa y ocho* (Madrid: Espasa Calpe, 1951). Tendentiously opposes inclusion of Valle-Inclán among *noventayochistas,* maintaining that Valle shows no real concern for the state of Spain in his later works.

_____. *Las estéticas de Valle-Inclán* (Madrid: Gredos, 1965). Considers three periods of Valle's works which he terms the mythical, the ironical and the degraded. Each is expressed through a particular character.

DIEGO, GERARDO. *Poesía española* (Madrid: Signo, 1934), pp. 83-85, 571-72. A selection of Valle's verse and some interesting observations by him on the nature of poetry.

DURAN, MANUEL. "La técnica de la novela y la generación del 98," *Revista Hispánica Moderna,* XXIII (1957), 14-27. Durán includes Valle among the *noventayochistas.* Observes shrewdly that at no point in his career did Valle create a fully rounded, credible character, because he passed directly from idealization to degradation.

FERNANDEZ ALMAGRO, MELCHOR. *Vida y literatura de Valle-Inclán* (Madrid: Nacional, 1943). A general study revised and reissued in 1966. Good for Valle's life, but necessarily brief in consideration of the works owing to its range.

FICHTER, WILLIAM. "Génesis de la *Sonata de estío,*" *Nueva Revista de Filología Hispánica* (Mexico), VII (1953), 3-4, 526-35. A detailed account of the genesis of the *Summer Sonata* which contributes to our knowledge of Valle's conception and elaboration of his novels as a whole.

————. *Publicaciones periodísticas de don Ramón del Valle-Inclán anteriores a 1895* (Mexico: El Colegio de Mexico, 1952). Indispensable for the understanding of the development of Valle-Inclán's writing. A long introduction with detailed comments on the newspaper articles and short stories Fichter has collected and published here.

FLYNN, GERARD COX. "The Adversary: Bradomín," *Hispanic Review,* XXIX (1961), 120-33. Considers the cultivated satanism of the marqués de Bradomín and concludes that his is essentially a diabolic nature.

FRANCO, J. "The Concept of Time in *El ruedo ibérico,*" *Bulletin of Hispanic Studies,* XXIX (1962), 177-87. A most important article in which for the first time the complex structure underlying the two completed novels of the *Iberian Ring* is analyzed. Also indicates Valle's interest in Gnosticism.

FUENTE, FRANCISCO DE LA. "Expresión de América y de los personajes americanos en Ramón del Valle-Inclán," *Humanidades* (La Plata), XXIX (1944), 104-16. Reprints Valle's poem "Nos vemos" about the Mexican Indian. Interesting comments on author's indifference to "realism" in terms of both landscape and character.

GHIRALDO, A. *El archivo de Rubén Darío* (Buenos Aires: Losada, 1943). Reprints four letters by Valle-Inclán.

GÓMEZ DE LA SERNA, GASPAR. "Las dos Españas de don Ramón del Valle-Inclán," *Clavileño* (Madrid), III, 17 (1952), 17-32. Essential to the understanding of Valle-Inclán's Carlism and the bitterness of his attitude towards the official Spain of Isabel II.

————. Prologue to Valle-Inclán's *Obras escogidas* (Madrid: Aguilar, 1958). Discusses the epic quality of Valle's works and his endeavor to move from the individual to the collective, from the lyric to the dramatic form.

GREENFIELD, SUMNER M. "Stylization and deformation in Valle-Inclán's *La reina castiza,*" *Bulletin of Hispanic Studies,* XXXIX (1962), 78-89. A shrewd analysis of important aspects of this farce and its place in the development of the *esperpento.*

GUERRERO ZAMORA, JUAN. *Historia del teatro contemporáneo,* I (Barcelona: Juan Flors, 1961), 153-206. An unusually sensitive and rewarding study of Valle-Inclán's theater.

LADO, MARÍA DOLORES. *Las guerras carlistas y el reinado isabelino en la obra Ramón del Valle-Inclán* (Gainesville, U. of Florida Press, 1966). An unpretentious but informative account of Valle's treatment of Spain in the nineteenth century.

LIVINGSTONE, LEON. "Interior Duplication in the Modern Spanish Novel," *PMLA,* Sept., 1958, 393-406. An absorbing study of some modern Spanish novelists, among them Pérez de Ayala and Valle-Inclán. Shows how novelists who scorn the base materials of reality in their fiction are forced to fall back on non-novelistic techniques, especially those of painting and music.

MADARIAGA, SALVADOR DE. *The Genius of Spain and other Essays* (Oxford: Humphrey Milford, 1930). Presents now outdated views, but which yet remain of interest as a personal and somewhat hostile assessment of Valle's pre-*esperpento* works.

MADRID, FRANCISCO. *La vida altiva de Valle-Inclán* (B. Aires: Poseidon, 1943). Concentrates on biography of author. There are also extracts from interviews and lectures in which Valle gives his views on various aspects of the writer's craft.

MARCH, MARÍA EUGENIA. *Forma e idea de los esperpentos de Valle-Inclán* (Madrid: Castalia, 1969). A general study of the *esperpentos* in which Valle-Inclán is described as an Expressionist writer.

MARÍAS, JULIÁN. *Valle-Inclán en el ruede ibérico* (Buenos Aires: Columba, 1967). A most stimulating analysis of Valle's attitude toward Spanish history in the nineteenth century.

MARRAST, ROBERT. "Algunas llaves para *Divinas palabras*," *Primer Acto* (Madrid), no. 46 (1963), 42-49. Considers the symmetrical structure of this play.

MARTÍNEZ SIERRA, G. "Hablanda con Valle-Inclán, de él y de su obra," *ABC*, 7 diciembre, 1928. An interview with Valle that sheds light on his theory of the *esperpento* and why he turned from plays to novels in the last stages of his writing career.

NENZIONI, GINO. "Gli *esperpentos* (a proposito del teatro di Ramón del Valle-Inclán)," *Letteratura Moderne*, IX (1959), 70-77 and 303-12. Considers that the *esperpento* does not involve a radical change in Valle's production, as is shown by his continued use of elements such as the macabre, superstitions, and the mingling of the grotesque and the wretched.

ORTEGA Y GASSET, JOSÉ. "*Sonata de estío*," *La Lectura* (Madrid), IV, 1 (1904), 227-33. A short but now famous review in which Ortega counsels Valle to abandon the 'cult of the princess" and devote his attention to more important questions.

RISCO, ANTONIO. *La estética de Valle-Inclán* (en los esperpentos y en "El ruedo ibérico"), (Madrid: Gredos, 1966). Risco's thesis is that Valle's attitude to society is totally negative. He is particularly enlightening on Valle's treatment of time and also on the grammatical aspects of his works.

RUBIA BARCIA, JOSÉ. "Valle-Inclán y la literatura gallega," *Revista Hispánica Moderna*, XXI, 2, 3, 4 (1955), 5-60. Rubia Barcia insists that Valle was not influenced by foreign writers, since many elements in his earlier fiction are present in Galician writers with whose work he would have been familiar. The tone of this article is marred by an all too apparent regional bias.

————. *A Bibliography and Iconography of Valle-Inclán* (Berkeley and Los Angeles: Univ. of California Press, 1960). Although, inevitably, the bibliography is now incomplete this is an indispensable work of reference.

SALINAS, PEDRO. "Significación del *esperpento* o Valle-Inclán hijo pródigo del '98." An unusually thought-provoking essay.

————. "Valle-Inclán visto por sus coetáneos." Contents are provocative, Ramiro de Maeztu's comments being of particular interest. Both these articles are in *Literatura española siglo XX* (Mexico: Robredo, 1949).

SEELEMEN, ROSA. "Folkloric elements in Valle-Inclán," *Hispanic Review*, III, (1935), 103-18. A detailed consideration of the superstitions, especially those of Galicia, which appear repeatedly in Valle's works.

SEGURA COVARSI, ENRIQUE. "Los ciegos en Valle-Inclán," *Clavileño* (Madrid), III, 17 (1952), 49-52. Notes how Valle-Inclán's veneration for the blind is a reflection of his philosophic beliefs, since for him sight implied what is mutable and transitory. Comments also on Valle's use of archetypes.

————. "*Cara de plata*," *Revista de literatura*, V, 9-10 (1954), 267-69. Dwells on the characters in this play and speaks in general terms of the collective characters who resemble the chorus in Greek tragedy.

SMITH, VERITY. *Valle-Inclán: Tirano Banderas* (London, Grant & Cutler, 1971). A short detailed study of the finest novel of Valle's maturity.

SPERATTI PIÑERO, EMMA SUSANA. *De 'Sonata de otoño' al Esperpento* (Aspectos del arte de Valle-Inclán), (London: Támesis, 1968). Includes all the most important of Professor Speratti's previously published articles on Valle-Inclán, together with her more detailed study of *Tirano Banderas*.

UMBRAL, FRANCISCO. *Valle-Inclán* (Madrid: Unión Editorial, 1968). A brief, perceptive and highly readable introduction to the writer and his works. It contains a few factual inaccuracies which, however, do not detract from its overall quality.

VALBUENA PRAT, ANGEL. *Historia de la literatura española*, III, (Barcelona: Gustavo Gili, 1953), 507-15. A brief, chronological survey of Valle-Inclán's works. Of particular interest for its quotation from a lecture given by Eugenio Montes in which Valle's debt to Plato is noted.

YNDURAIN, FRANCISCO. *Valle-Inclán: tres estudios* (Santander: La Isla de los Ratones, 1969). Three short, lucid and perceptive essays devoted exclusively to *La corte de los milagros* and *Viva mi dueño*.

ZAHAREAS, ANTHONY (ed.). *Ramón del Valle-Inclán: An Appraisal of his Life and Works* (New York: Las Américas, 1968). A very comprehensive and wide-ranging survey of Valle-Inclán's works including articles of considerable quality. The various contributions cover every phase of Valle's career from *Modernismo* through to the *esperpento* and his later return to the novel.

ZAHAREAS, ANTHONY AND CARDONA, RODOLFO. *Visión del esperpento* (teoría y práctica en los esperpentos de Valle-Inclán), (Madrid: Castalia, 1970). A detailed, well-documented but slightly labored analysis of the *esperpentos* in dramatic form.

ZAMORA VICENTE, A. *La realidad esperpéntica* (aproximación a "Luces de bohemia"), (Madrid: Gredos, 1969). A very detailed analysis of this play. Among the facets considered are language, possible sources and the element of social and political protest.

_____. *Las Sonatas de Ramón del Valle-Inclán* (Madrid: Gredos, 1955). A classic study of the *modernista* elements in the four *Sonatas* in which attention is given to the appeal to the senses, theatrical techniques, landscape, superstitions and ideology.

    .   .   .   .

Some centennial studies and special numbers of journals devoted to Valle-Inclán.

Cuadernos Hispanoamericanos (Madrid), nos. 199-200 (July-Aug., 1966). Contains a total of thirty-one articles on numerous aspects of Valle's work. Among the contributors are Robert Marrast, A. Zamora Vicente, Luis Granjel and J. M. Blecua.

La Pluma (Madrid), IV, no. 32 (January 1923). Includes articles by Pérez de Ayala, Antonio Machado, Alfonso Reyes, Ricardo Baroja and other contemporaries.

Insula (Madrid), nos. 236-37 (July-Aug., 1966). Contains interesting contributions by Speratti Piñero, Francisco Yndurain, Manuel Durán and others on Valle's later works, together with articles of biographical interest.

Papeles de Son Armadans (Palma de Mallorca), XLIII, no. 127 (Oct., 1966). Particularly recommended is Ricardo Gullón's article on *Tirano Banderas*, "Técnicas de Valle-Inclán."

Ramón del Valle-Inclán (1866-1966). (Universidad Nacional de La Plata, 1967). Consists of an introduction followed by five separate sections, each one of these being concerned with a particular facet of the author. Of particular interest are the reporters' summaries of the four lectures Valle delivered in Buenos Aires in 1910. These are given by Aurelia C. Garat at the end of her article "Valle-Inclán en la Argentina."

Revista de Occidente (Madrid), nos. 44-5 (November-Dec., 1966). Particularly recommended are García Pelayo's article about the social world in Valle's works, and the correspondence between Valle, Clarín and Palacio Valdés reproduced by Gamallo Fierros.

Index

(The works of Valle-Inclán are listed under his name)